A PARENT'S WORST NIGHTMARE

THE IMPACT OF
THC
ON OUR CHILDREN

D1715684

STORIES COMPILED BY
LAURA STACK

JOHNNYSAMBASSADORS.ORG

The Impact of THC on Our Children: A Parent's Worst Nightmare

Compiled by Laura Stack
Written by Johnny's Ambassadors

All proceeds on the sale of this book go to Johnny's Ambassadors, a 501(c)(3) nonprofit in Colorado.

Published by Johnny's Ambassadors Publishing.
4242 Hickory Oaks Street, Castle Rock, CO 80104
JohnnysAmbassadors.org

ISBN 9798322701262

Printed in the United States of America.

This book is dedicated to its 24 authors (one parent has two children).
Each story is captivating and heartbreaking.
I give these parents so much credit, love, and gratitude for being
willing to share their painful experiences to help others.

CONTENTS

INTRODUCTION:
JOHNNY STACK'S LIFE
AND DEATH STORY

JOHN KENNETH STACK was born in Littleton, Colorado, on February 7, 2000, and died on November 20, 2019, in Lone Tree, Colorado. We called him Johnny because my husband is also named John. Johnny was a sweet, intelligent, happy child. He participated in many sports and took piano and guitar lessons. As a child, every night he wanted me to read with him, pray with him, and sing lullabies while rubbing his back as he fell asleep.

Johnny had a spirit of service and a kind heart. He was a loyal friend and a loving son. He had a 4.0 GPA and earned a scholarship to Colorado State University. He was a regular kid in a regular, loving family.

As most parents do, we often told our children, "Don't do drugs of any kind, ever. Drugs will ruin your brain. If you never try it, you'll never get hooked, etc., etc., etc."

Unfortunately, we live in Colorado, which was the first state to legalize recreational marijuana in 2012. It became available in dispensaries in 2014 when Johnny was 14 years old. He first tried marijuana at a high school party. I know because he told us. He came home and said there was marijuana at the party, and all the boys wanted to try to get high. He felt pressured to try it and didn't know what to say, and so, he did.

Many parents think their children start using THC (delta-9-tetrahy-drocannabinol, the psychoactive chemical in marijuana) to combat life's stressors or because they think marijuana isn't as dangerous as other drugs. Maybe these young people see their friends use it, and they haven't had any problems. Perhaps they're just curious. Or, like Johnny, perhaps they like getting high with their friends, so they get hooked and can't stop. At this early point in his use, I had no idea about the potency and addiction potential of today's THC products, such as dabs, vapes, and gummies. I didn't understand adolescent brain development. I didn't know high-potency marijuana could trigger or cause mental illness.

Dabbing means inhaling the vapors of a concentrated THC product, where the THC has been extracted from the plant. Dabbing is highly addictive, but it doesn't take an addiction for dabbing to hurt you. It can take just one hit to put someone in the hospital with acute psychosis. My 51-year-old girlfriend landed in a mental hospital from hallucinations caused by hitting a dab pen twice. This doesn't even account for all the damage to users' families—often accidentally, sometimes fatally. Using THC can also cause mental illness, slowly, over years of heavy use, especially in adolescents. (See the research in the appendices in the back of this book.)

Maybe you think young users are just being typical teens. Maybe you think marijuana is harmless because it's legal. Maybe you think your child is getting straight A's, so marijuana can't affect them, or it can't happen in your family because you go to church. I used to think all of that too, but numerous medical studies show THC use can slow mental development, cause depression, and lead to schizophrenia. These mental illnesses can lead to suicide.

In Johnny's junior year of high school, he had his first "real" girlfriend. In a seven-month period, he went from being a nice, sweet kid to being a jerk to her. His marijuana use led him to treat her and all his friends poorly. Several of his friends came up to me at the funeral, apologetically saying, "Johnny and I weren't on speaking terms at the end."

He continued to get A's in school but started procrastinating and didn't seem motivated to learn. He played a lot of video games. Knowing he was interested in becoming a game designer, computer programmer, or computer engineer, I didn't say much when he isolated himself in his room.

Johnny was skillful at hiding his marijuana use from us. We found out later from Snapchat photos that the little cartridges he told us contained nicotine really contained THC distillates. He was refilling them and using THC right under our noses. We were clueless that it was THC.

One morning, I went into his room before school and saw a telltale haze in the air.

"Johnny," I said, "you know there is no vaping allowed in the house!"

"Mom, it's no big deal," he replied. "Everyone does it."

I told John what happened, and while Johnny was at school, we searched his room. We found a glass pipe and a small butane torch, like one you'd use for crème brûlée.

We confronted him when he came home. "Johnny, do you have an explanation for these items?"

"Those aren't mine," Johnny said. "They're my friend's."

John took the pipe out to the cement patio and smashed it. Then we grounded Johnny and took away his car for a time. His disobedience only escalated. John bought a car tracker. Johnny's stories of what he was doing, who he was with, and where he was going didn't add up. We took away his car again, so he refused to go to school, and his grades started to slip. He thought we were tracking his phone, but he didn't know about the car tracker for a long time. When he found it, he smashed it on the driveway.

One night, he was driving his brother, James, home from baseball practice. He drove into a construction zone, and the cones suddenly narrowed from two lanes to one. He was going too fast and hit the car in front of him.

Everyone was fine physically, but the cars were totaled. It's likely he was high. He could have killed everyone in both cars. I didn't know until later that Johnny routinely drove while high. His therapist told me Johnny had driven to his office for an appointment while high. After Johnny passed, I discovered Snapchat videos on his phone he took of himself driving and hitting his pen with his friends in the car. It broke my heart to learn my son had put his friends in danger.

Johnny's whole personality changed. He became moody and lacked motivation. He no longer wanted to participate in any extracurricular activities and kept withdrawing to his bedroom to be alone and play his games. His attitude was basically that he was getting straight A's, so he wanted to be left alone. This was what he wanted to do for a living. He became increasingly irritable. He stopped doing his chores and no longer followed household rules. He would stand defiantly in the hallway and vape. At times, he would complain of random stomach pain and stayed home from school.

You might be wondering how I missed all of this. I simply thought he was being a hormonal teenager. Not having experience with marijuana, I didn't recognize he was having a problem with it or how much he was using.

The first semester of his senior year, Johnny got a perfect 800 SAT score in the math section. As a parent, it was easy to rationalize. I'd think, *He did well on these assessments, so he can't be having problems.* Or *He's getting straight A's, has a 4.0 GPA, and got a scholarship, so maybe the marijuana isn't affecting him much.* By the end of his senior year, after nearly failing the last semester with four D's, his GPA was still so high he graduated with honors. Don't let good grades fool you! His situation worsened significantly. He was now getting into legal trouble from his acting out.

The night of his high school homecoming, he failed to come home. I assumed he couldn't because he was high. He walked breezily into the house the following morning as if nothing had happened. This time, we took the car away for three days. He argued with us about it, and when we refused to give the car back, he went up to his room, packed his suitcase, and left.

We didn't know where he went. One mom reached out to me about letting him stay with her. That lasted only one night because he got into a fight with a good friend. We got concerned when we didn't hear from him for several days. The phone tracker app showed him up in north Denver at an unknown location, which we now assume was a marijuana dealer. With the help of his therapist, on September 27, 2017, we wrote Johnny an ultimatum letter. We let him know we were cutting him off financially, and he would not have access to our home if he did not return home by October 2 at 8:00 p.m. At 8:02 p.m., Johnny calmly walked through the door. "I will agree to follow the rules," he said. One of the rules was drug testing; however, we didn't follow through on it, which is a big regret of mine.

In the second semester of his senior year, Johnny continued to be defiant and started missing school. At the beginning of the semester, he told his counselor he would be 18 soon, so I couldn't require him to attend school as he'd be an adult. He advised the school to discontinue our access to his school portal, so we couldn't see his grades or how much school he was missing. More than anything I wanted Johnny to finish high school. I remember thinking, *We just need to get through high school. He will graduate, go to college on his scholarship, meet some new people, and he will be okay.*

As a last-ditch effort to get him to attend school regularly and do his homework, we confiscated his laptop. We told him he was to use the desktop in my office for his homework. He wasn't allowed to play his video games until his grades and attendance had improved. He got so angry that he got physical. He entered my bedroom, demanded his laptop back, and shoved me. John was in the master bathroom. As he turned the corner, he saw the entire action. John has a second-degree black belt in karate, so Johnny found himself flat on his back in about two seconds. John yelled at him and told him he was never to put his hands on me again. This was clearly a volatile situation.

The following morning when Johnny was in the shower, we searched through his backpack and found a glass pipe. We confronted him. I broke the pipe and threw it away. Johnny swore at me, calling me the worst names I'd ever heard. Hearing that, I had a bit of a meltdown and started sobbing.

We installed locks on our bedroom doors when Johnny became more erratic and mean. It was simply not safe to have him in the home, especially with our younger son still living at home. So, when he turned 18, we helped him find a room to rent close to us and his school. I wish we had known about sober living facilities or therapeutic boarding schools back then.

We didn't have access to Johnny's phone, so we couldn't see the selfie he took of himself a few weeks later, driving to get his "medical" marijuana card. A friend confirmed Johnny had received a "medical" marijuana card and bought his high-potency THC distillates from a dispensary. She said he hit a small dab pen throughout the day. He had another small water pipe he used for solid concentrates.

Once we obtained access to his phone, we could get into his other devices, computers, and apps. We were shocked at the information that we found. One photo was of him driving three other young adolescents who looked to be 13 or 14—the same age Johnny was when he started using marijuana. Johnny had come full circle. He had become the local school marijuana dealer. Most of the photos were selfies using marijuana and his "friends" using marijuana. There were also photos of THC products and stacks of money, confirming he also started dealing.

So, does a regulated pot industry keep marijuana away from our 18-year-old kids? NO! The opposite is true. It allows them to deal drugs to younger kids. No black market needed. Teens can't get tobacco or alcohol legally, but they can obtain a medical marijuana card at 18 without parental knowledge or approval. Then they just need to find a "pot shop" doctor who will write a recommendation if you complain of a headache and thereby sacrifice the minds and souls of children for a few hundred dollars.

The bottom line is the "pot shop" situation in Colorado is like the "pill mills" in the opioid crisis. Kids can pay a few hundred bucks and get a medical marijuana card for some made-up ailment all for the single purpose of getting high. Johnny lied and said he had migraines because there's no way to prove it. (Teens teach each other to say this.)

Johnny stopped going to school altogether. His counselor and I stayed in close contact about what Johnny needed to do to graduate. I would nag him about it, and sometimes I got him to turn in assignments. That semester, he had 21 unexcused absences and 35 total absences in 87 days.

We would invite him to dinner periodically to check in with him and feed him a home-cooked meal. One night, he made a big announcement: "I just love marijuana. I'm going to smoke marijuana for the rest of my life!" He said marijuana made him feel great, and he was automatically accepted by those who used it. I found out through our younger son that Johnny had lost his "real" friends due to the choices he was making. Almost none of them were on speaking terms any longer, so he had to create new "friends" whose only connection was smoking weed together. Smoking was the only way he felt like he belonged.

I asked him repeatedly to let me help him stop the marijuana, but he would say, "Mom, I'm fine. Leave me alone." He wasn't fine. His school counselor called me to say that if Johnny didn't take his English final, he would not earn the D he needed to graduate. Despite his resistance, I made sure Johnny graduated. Johnny marched across the stage with his honor cords flowing, looking happy. Except for his unkempt long hair that clearly hadn't been cut in months, there's no way you could know he was a marijuana addict.

He went to Colorado State University (CSU) and dabbed nonstop with his roommate for two weeks. He texted me that he felt like killing himself every day. He went to a mental hospital for suicidality and was diagnosed with "THC Abuse—Severe." He lost his scholarship to CSU and moved back home. He stopped using THC, recovered, and was sober for several months.

Then he received a scholarship to the University of Northern Colorado (UNC) and started vaping and dabbing again. A few months later, he called me at 3 a.m. and said his dorm room was bugged and claimed UNC was an FBI base. He went back to the mental hospital for cannabis-induced psychosis and went on an antipsychotic. He lost the scholarship to UNC, so we moved him into our condo down the road. He got a job at PetSmart and a new puppy, Benji, and seemed to be recovering with sobriety.

Sadly, he got back together with an old bad-news girlfriend, who got him dabbing wax again, which we didn't know. They got in a fight, and she punched him. He suddenly had a "come to Jesus" moment, where he realized his life had been ruined by THC, and he swore off it. Unfortunately, he also stopped taking his antipsychotic without tapering off, and we suspect the delusional thoughts about the FBI came back.

One Sunday, John and I had gone to church and had invited Johnny to go with us. That evening, he came over at 5:30 p.m. for dinner. "Johnny!" I said, greeting him joyfully at the front door.

He said, "I'd like to go to church now." I was happy and thought, *This is fantastic! He hasn't been to church in a long time.*

I said, "Johnny, church was at 11 a.m. this morning. Services are all over for the day."

Then Johnny said, "I guess it's too late for me."

Did he mean it was too late to come back to the Lord?

"Oh, Johnny," I said, "it's never too late, and you don't have to go to church to ask the Lord back into your life. Just ask Jesus to forgive your sins, make a commitment to live for Him, and ask Him to sit on the throne of your life." Johnny was happy with that response and seemed relieved.

Then, standing in the kitchen, Johnny turned to me and pointedly said, "Mom, I want you to know you were right. You told me marijuana would hurt my brain. Marijuana has ruined my mind and my life. I'm sorry, and I love you." He hugged me, and I was so happy he wanted to settle things between us. He could be vicious during his psychotic episodes, and our relationship had been strained for many years. I used to be "his person" and loved him unconditionally. I didn't see this act of reconciliation as a suicidal indicator, but it probably was, and I missed it.

Johnny asked us to meet him at Red Robin on November 18, 2019, at 6:00 p.m. "I have something I need to talk to you about," he said. At 6:30, John and I were still waiting for him to show up. We had already ordered his favorite Royal Red Robin burger and Oreo Cookie Magic Milkshake for him. When he finally arrived, he ate a little bit and suddenly announced his news: "I need to move to California."

"Wait, what?" I asked. "Why?"

"I need to get out of Highlands Ranch. I've got to get away from everyone here. What will happen to my dog?"

"You'll take him with you wherever you go," I said. "He's your dog. You'll figure out where to work and how to take care of him."

Johnny exclaimed, "You're the worst parents in the world!" He got up and stormed out of the restaurant. John and I looked at each other, mouths open.

On November 19, 2019, Johnny showed up at our house without calling. "I owe you a huge apology," he said. "I do not know what I was thinking. I've been an idiot. I don't know how to say it other than that."

Johnny had the next day off work, and I wanted to give him some space, so we did not talk. My cell phone rang at 1:03 a.m., on Thursday, November 21, 2019. I always kept my ringtone volume at full blast, so I would be sure to awaken to Johnny's late-night calls. I reached over to pick up the phone, fully expecting to see Johnny's name on the screen. Instead, it said Douglas County Sheriff's Office.

"Hello?"

"Hello, ma'am, I'm with the Douglas County Sheriff's Office. I'm at your front door. Will you please come down and let us in?"

I asked, "Do you have Johnny with you?"

"No, ma'am. I'm sorry … I do not."

A cold chill slithered through my veins. I rolled over and shook John's shoulder. "John," I said, "wake up. The police are at the door. It's Johnny again."

My husband jumped out of bed. We threw on our robes and hurried downstairs. John yanked open the door. A uniformed police officer stood there with a woman in a black shirt and pants. We motioned for them to come inside and led them into the living room.

The woman in black said, "Mr. and Mrs. Stack, I'm with the coroner's office. I'm so sorry to tell you that your son is deceased."

I stared at her for a few seconds. "Deceased? What do you mean—deceased?"

"He's dead, ma'am. He jumped off the roof of the RTD parking garage on Park Meadows Drive."

I heard myself screaming as I fell into John's arms. And then for the next few moments, I heard nothing.

My conversation with Johnny flashed into my mind. *"Mom, I just want you to know you were right. You told me marijuana would hurt my brain. Marijuana has ruined my mind and my life. I'm sorry, and I love you."* In the end, he knew it was marijuana that had caused his problems.

John and I began living every parent's nightmare. While I sat wailing against John's chest, he held me tight and tried to talk to the police officer and the coroner. He explained about Johnny's THC use and cannabis-induced mental illness. After the coroner and police had finished their reports and paperwork, they told us how sorry they were one final time, and they departed. John and I stared at each other, fell into each other's arms, and held each other, wailing.

Unquestionably, this is a very painful memory. For many months, I had recurring nightmares. I would wake up in a cold sweat. Some nights, after not being able to get out of bed from crying all day, I was so deeply depressed that I didn't know if I could make it another night. Sometimes, I asked God why He did not take me instead. John, my children, family, friends, and the Lord got me through those dark times.

I had periods of anger. I was angry at the marijuana industry. I was angry at the attorneys, the lobbyists, and the legislators who helped legalize marijuana in Colorado so my boy could access it. I was angry at myself for not moving to Idaho or somewhere else where it was still illegal. I was angry at the growers, the dispensary owners, and the manufacturers of this poison. I was angry at Johnny for using it. Johnny's decision to use marijuana led to addiction and psychosis, but it shouldn't have been as readily available as it was. In the end, the blame for Johnny's death lies squarely on marijuana; without it, Johnny would still be here.

I have stopped blaming myself. It has taken me a long time to get to this point. We weren't perfect parents, but John and I did the best we could with what we knew.

You can read Johnny's entire story in my first book I wrote six months after he died, *The Dangerous Truth About Today's Marijuana: Johnny Stack's Life and Death Story.*

There is no scenario in which cannabis is guaranteed to be harmless for anybody. If you know your child is genetically inclined or already has a mental illness, mood disorder, or genetic predisposition, keep your child away from marijuana. If your child has none of these things, keep your child away from marijuana. Having certain genes does not automatically cause schizophrenia. Dr. Erik Messamore, a member of the Johnny's Ambassadors Scientific Advisory Board, said, "Genetics aren't destiny. You can protect them to avoid mental illness." Genes usually require a trigger—an environmental change that pushes them over the edge. Marijuana often provides that trigger.

Eventually, when someone has repeated cannabis-induced psychosis (CIP) incidents, the psychosis may not go away. Johnny's psychiatrist diagnosed him with schizoaffective disorder but never gave him the label of schizophrenia, since Johnny didn't have psychosis for the requisite six months. During periods of sobriety, Johnny's delusional thinking would subside, but it would come roaring back with THC use.

When Johnny was having issues with THC, there was nowhere to turn. There was no one to talk to. There were no cannabis treatment programs.

The doctors didn't take us seriously about Johnny's THC addiction. There was little understanding of cannabis-induced psychosis. I knew it was up to me to share my story with others.

So, six months after Johnny died, in May 2020, I founded the nonprofit Johnny's Ambassadors Youth THC Prevention (JohnnysAmbassadors. org) to try to change what I could and keep other families from going through this horror. We are determined to keep young people from following Johnny's path. This is how I can make a difference, honor Johnny's life, and keep his spirit alive. I now speak at over 200 student assemblies each year at middle and high schools around the U.S., teaching hundreds of thousands of teens about the harms of THC misuse. I share Johnny's warning with them: "Marijuana ruined my mind and my life." I believe Johnny told me because he knew I would go and tell these young people what he said.

As of this writing, we have more than 12,000 Johnny's Ambassadors around the globe, helping us educate parents, teens, and communities about the dangers of today's potent THC products (marijuana, dabs, vapes, and edibles) on adolescent brain development and their connection to psychosis and suicide.

These are some of the stories from members of our private Parents of Children with Cannabis-Induced Psychosis (POCCIP) Facebook group. There are thousands more untold.

You are not alone. We understand. If you're worried about your teen's THC use, please reach out to me for help at Laura@JohnnysAmbassadors. org.

CHAPTER 1:

"It's Just Weed. It's Pretty Harmless, Right?"

"IT'S JUST WEED. It's pretty harmless, right?" Those are words I spoke to my husband one night in the spring of 2022 when we thought our 23-year-old son seemed high. Prior to that night, I had no idea my son had ever smoked or vaped anything, even nicotine! My sweet middle child was so intelligent, responsible, thoughtful, and kind. Tall, athletic, handsome by anyone's standards. Everyone liked him instantly. His teachers would tell me what a joy he was to have in class, and they knew he would go on to do great things in life. He was an honors student, a computer whiz, a soccer player, and an all-around good guy. He had many lifelong friends, mostly kids who would fall into the nerd or geek category—the "smart kids." I never worried about him experimenting with drinking or smoking because he and his friends were such trustworthy, sensible kids.

High school flowed effortlessly into college, and my son was thrilled to be accepted into the large state university here in our hometown in Florida. He had no interest in living in a dorm, opting instead to continue living at home and driving to campus each day. He seemed to be doing fine at college, and I didn't feel any need to be a helicopter parent and monitor his grades or his whereabouts.

By the end of his sophomore year, though, he said he was struggling in some classes and was feeling a lot of anxiety. We told him we could get him tutors if needed, and not to worry because everything would be fine. We didn't see very much of him, as he would come home from school and retreat to his room when he didn't have plans with his friends. It all seemed normal, considering his age and the circumstances.

My husband would sometimes get out of bed at 3 or 4 a.m. to get a drink of water and would bump into our son in the hallway, still up. We knew he had a lot of studying to do and papers to write, so even that was easy to explain away.

In 2022, we discovered he was in real academic trouble and had failed many classes due to a marijuana addiction, which had caused a complete loss of motivation. He also suffered from cannabinoid hyperemesis syndrome (repeated and severe vomiting caused by marijuana use) and would stay in his car smoking weed and puking into a bag all day rather than go to class. Then he would stay up all night vaping THC instead of sleeping.

One night at home our son came downstairs in the early evening to hang out with us. We thought he seemed a little drunk, which was strange, but we assumed he might have tried alcohol to deal with the stress of school. The following weekend was Mother's Day, and he showed up with a card and flowers. He said he'd been out all night with friends and hadn't slept. My husband and I both said to each other later, "Wow, he seemed high, didn't he?" Although we both agreed that even if he was high, it was just weed, and that was nothing to really worry about.

A week later, he and some of his friends were planning to work at a festival in a town an hour from our home. At the last minute, my husband and I decided to go to the festival as well and to make a fun weekend of it. We texted him to tell him to keep an eye out for us, so we could say hello when we bumped into one another. We got to the festival and saw him working, but he looked and seemed a little off. When we made our way over to him after his shift was over, he asked me if he could speak to me alone. We walked around the corner, and he began to tell me his friends had all tried to molest him the night before. He claimed his friends' parents were running a big pedophile ring. I was so confused! He almost seemed like his "normal" self, yet he was making no sense. Then he told me he was a Buddhist, completely enlightened and just wanted me to seek to understand him. He explained he knew so much more about God and life and the universe than everyone else. Then, fearfully, he asked if my husband and I would help him escape and get him away from his friends before they hurt him.

I was still very confused, but all I could think of to explain the bizarre behavior was maybe he had been given LSD or magic mushrooms or some sort of psychedelic drugs that made him hallucinate. We helped him gather his things and put him in the car with us and took him home. We thought if he slept it off, he would sober up and would act normal again. In the morning, he still seemed a bit off, but he was not nearly as bad as the night before.

I looked through his car while he slept to see if I could find any drugs or evidence of what had made him act so strangely. Sure enough, I found an unopened box with a vape device inside printed with "Delta-8," and some other empty boxes of Delta-8 vapes in different flavors. I had never heard of Delta-8 and had no clue what it was. A Google search revealed posts stating it was a milder form of THC made from hemp—safe and organic. However, when I googled "bad effects of Delta-8," I found hundreds of articles, threads, and posts talking about the risks of psychosis. I read how some people experienced such a "bad trip" from smoking Delta-8 vapes or eating Delta-8 gummies, they couldn't get up out of bed for days, suffering from hallucinations and confusion. They often saw demons and thought they had died or were dying.

That morning, we had a long talk with our son about the dangers of vaping this stuff, and of course, he said he understood. Later, he said he had to run an errand and was gone for only a few minutes. Then he came back and went up to his room. The next morning, he came down and was out of his mind, acting even more strangely than the night before. He had smoked THC all night and again was saying things that made absolutely no sense, like a person with paranoid schizophrenia. He said we were out to get him, and all his friends were out to get him.

He deleted all his social media, namely Snapchat, which he used to communicate with his friends. He said we were all against him because he was transgender.

"When did you decide you were transgender?" we asked. "Do you want to be a woman? Dress like a woman?"

"No," he said, but he didn't want to be a man anymore because men could not be trusted. He had the craziest look in his eyes. He had a strange voice that didn't sound like his own.

He became increasingly agitated, darted out the front door, and began running up the street. I chased after him in the car and asked him to get in so we could talk and work things out, but he refused and said he never wanted to see me again. His dad was able to coax him into his car by promising him he wouldn't have to go home or talk to me. In the meantime, I called two of his best friends to explain to them what was going on and see what they would tell me about his drug use. I pleaded with them to be honest with me, so we could get my son treatment and help him get back to his normal, sweet self. They both explained they had all smoked "regular marijuana" for a long time and then had started using Delta-8 vapes a few months ago.

My husband was able to get our son to the emergency department (ED) by telling him we thought he had hepatitis and needed to get some liver tests run. Somehow, in his delusional state, this made sense to him, so he agreed to go. I drove there separately, and once inside, explained to the hospital staff we had just discovered he was a heavy smoker of marijuana and Delta-8, and he was experiencing THC-induced psychosis.

While assessing my son, they asked him his name and what the date was. Because he was able to answer, they were going to let him leave. I had to beg and plead for them to help us and admit him, because our wonderful son had lost his mind, was psychotic, and needed treatment. About a minute later, the psychosis reared its ugly head again, and he started acting erratically and shouting things that made no sense. Our son tried to escape by running out into the street, but hospital security was able to catch him and take him back inside. He became loud and belligerent, and the guards were forced to restrain him. A short time later, the hospital staff Baker Acted him, as he was obviously a danger to himself and others. They allowed me and my 25-year-old daughter to stay with him in the room where he was held for the night.

Much to my surprise, the ED doctors told me people come in daily with psychosis from Delta-8 or wax "dabs" and other marijuana products. My immediate thought was, *Why aren't the hospitals making the public aware and alerting the government, so the manufacturers and distributors can be shut down and have this poison banned?* The doctors explained recovery from THC psychosis is a very long and difficult process, and some people never recover and are left with schizophrenia. They said this high-potency THC changes the brain.

By the way, the hospital lab tests showed only THC, no other drugs in my son's system! His friends told me the weed and Delta-8 vapes must have been "laced," because nobody believed THC products could do this to someone. They were so wrong! THC alone was responsible for the psychosis.

Once in his hospital room, he began acting bizarrely again, shouting out and begging the doctors for some Delta-8. He was shaking, sweating, and writhing in the bed like a person addicted to heroin or meth. He explained to the doctor when the withdrawal starts, he must always smoke more to make the shaking stop. He was catatonic at one point, sitting on the bed with a blank stare, appearing unable to see or hear us. It was a long night full of horrific experiences—ones I wish my sweet daughter and I never had to witness.

The next morning, they transferred my son by ambulance to a psychiatric hospital. I drove there and sat with him in a locked waiting room with a few other patients with addictions or mentally ill patients, none of whom had a family member or friend with them. In a six-hour period, not once did anyone check on or ask about my son or any of the other patients. Someone was watching through a two-way mirror, but none of the patients were spoken to or offered anything, such as a drink of water or a bed to lie on. During this time, my son asked me, literally about every 30 seconds, "Did I die?" in that strange voice that didn't sound like his own. I had to hold him up, or he would have slumped over onto the floor. At one point he looked me in the eye and said, "Who are you again?" He absolutely did not recognize me or know I was his mother.

After they took him to his new room at the psychiatric hospital, I couldn't see him again for three days. He called me several times saying, "Mom, did I die? Am I dead?" He was starting to come around slowly but was clearly still very confused. They diagnosed him with THC-induced psychosis. After three days, they sent him home, after I proved I had enrolled him in either an inpatient drug treatment center or an intensive outpatient program (IOP). We chose an IOP. He was given a prescription for an antipsychotic drug. It did seem to help him start to come out of psychosis, but after about two weeks, he said it made him feel terrible and didn't want to take it anymore.

We consulted with our regular family doctor and a psychiatrist we found online, who met with us via Zoom, because none of the local psychiatrists we contacted had immediate availability. The doctors agreed he could stop the antipsychotic, as long as he stayed clean from THC and continued his IOP treatment. After stopping the antipsychotic, he experienced another bad psychotic episode lasting a few days. He continued his IOP, which consisted of both one-on-one treatment with a drug counselor and group therapy sessions.

Beating the addiction was essential to him standing a chance to heal his brain and get his life back. We drug tested him at home to keep him accountable, and they also drug tested him at the treatment center. We took his car away, as well as his cell phone, Xbox, and laptop. They would have made it too tempting to order marijuana or Delta-8 products online and have them secretly delivered to the house. He was not allowed to see any of his old friends or go anywhere other than the treatment center or the gym.

As weeks went by, because he remained committed to his recovery and stayed sober, we allowed him to have his phone back, and many weeks later, his car. He slowly started to heal, but I do feel he had brain damage because he showed a noticeable loss of IQ and cognitive abilities during the first year after psychosis. He slept a lot, and his personality was very flat. It took about eight months before he started to act somewhat like his old self.

There are many horrific details I've left out of what our son experienced and what our family endured due to the THC poisoning and its devastating effects. I'm so angry these harmful toxic products are sold legally! I've seen reports of lab tests showing Delta-8 vapes contain products such as floor cleaners! It is completely unregulated. Anybody can set up a makeshift factory in a warehouse or a home and put chemicals in a vape cartridge and label it as Delta-8 or whatever in pretty packaging and sell it in vape shops. Your kids could be vaping bleach or acid! Everyone needs to be made aware of how many thousands of people are being harmed by these products. Recently, I've noticed a disturbing new trend of kava shops offering Delta-8 shots in their coffees and teas.

People need to know how these products can damage their brains! The results can be catastrophic! If data were released from all the hospitals and emergency departments, I know people would be shocked at how many are being harmed by the new, super high-potency THC. Law enforcement personnel also need to be made aware of this new epidemic. The legalization of marijuana is giving people a false perception that it's safe. This could not be further from the truth! These products are likely to blame for many violent crimes where young people are overcome suddenly with "mental illness." Many of them are likely to become psychotic from consuming toxic vapes and edibles.

America needs to see the facts and admit the truth … it's not "just weed." It's so much more potent now than it used to be, it's a different drug altogether, and it's destroying lives. For parents and families of loved ones addicted to THC and experiencing the horrors of psychosis, treatment is almost impossible to find and even harder to financially afford. We are very fortunate our son, with over a year of drug counseling behind him and a commitment to staying drug-free, is going to be okay. Many others suffering from psychosis are not so fortunate and die by suicide or are left with schizophrenia.

I beg everyone to hear our stories and help raise awareness about the devastation high-potency THC causes, so we can prevent others from going through the horror we have been through.

CHAPTER 2:

How Do You Get Your Kid Back After THC Use?

THE SUMMER OF 2018 brought one of the worst nightmares we could have ever imagined. What was planned as a relaxing family vacation turned into pure terror when our son experienced his first psychotic episode. It was unlike anything I had ever witnessed before. This episode was the beginning of a journey into mental health hospitals, learning about the effects of marijuana concentrates, psychosis, mental health, and bipolar disorder—all stemming from the legal, harmless, recreational, and socially acceptable use of weed.

Our son has always been a creative, playful, loving, and very sensitive kid. When starting high school, he felt the pressure of being "in," which meant being part of a popular group of kids. He was bullied and criticized, and I believe he couldn't figure out how to be okay with just being "okay." Trying to tell him that one day high school would be over, and he wouldn't care as much what others thought, simply did not resonate with his teenage brain.

He started using marijuana when he began hanging out with a new group of friends who were not as critical of him. We started noticing a change in his dressing style but just thought he was going through another teenager phase. In his last year of high school, we discovered he was using marijuana.

That year was rough: a lot of outbursts, holes punched in walls, and late nights waiting for him to get home from another party. We walked on eggshells for fear of tripping his anxieties and unleashing his temper.

We tried counseling at this point. We met with a psychiatrist to start some medication that could help with the outbursts and a therapist to talk about ways to cope and the effects of marijuana. We took classes to help each other communicate as a family.

We tried setting boundaries. We signed contracts, bought test kits, and tried enforcing consequences. However, we found following up is easier said than done when you are not in control, or able to lead or manage. He had a job, which was good, but we found out later he was smoking marijuana with some coworkers in the parking lot at the end of his shifts. He was skipping school a lot at this stage. He went from being recognized in middle school for academic excellence and taking college classes in high school to almost failing to get his high school diploma. He did graduate, though, and was accepted into college. We kept hoping we could get over this phase and college would bring a different motivation.

As soon as he turned 18, he went to get a medical marijuana card. I was able to contact the prescribing doctor's office. They said they couldn't talk to me because he was now considered an adult. I was horrified.

Little did we know, the beginning of the nightmare began when our son started dabbing. He used a form of concentrated THC called "wax." We were unaware these products existed or that he had started using them. We realized only later that he was using it daily, even at home while we were at work.

In the summer of 2018 at the start of vacation, things seemed okay, although he was a little fragile and exhibited a few strange behaviors and mood swings. Our son talked about how he really liked marijuana. He thought it wasn't a bad thing because no one had ever overdosed and died because of it. I tried listening, but I was having a really hard time. Ever since state legislation legalized marijuana, it seemed to have been so normalized, with dispensaries everywhere and many adults using it for recreational purposes.

It was during a family outing on that vacation the first psychotic episode occurred. We felt blindsided and bewildered. It was as though our son was a completely different person we did not know, and we were clueless as to what to do. We ended up in an emergency department and naïvely thought it might just be a matter of taking some medications and a couple of days to get back on track. What we didn't know was it would be the start of a new reality and learning about the relationship between THC, psychosis, and mental health.

My son was transferred to a bigger hospital with a mental health unit. When he checked in, there were still remnants of marijuana in his system— no other drugs. It was so hard to leave him at the hospital. He did not want to stay, but we knew we could not keep him safe. His beliefs and paranoia were making him do unsafe things. He was awake at all hours of the night. He was not eating. He was truly anxious and upset and thought things that were not real had meaning. For example, he received calls from a credit card telemarketer, and he thought it was a special coded way for him to receive messages from a celebrity he used to follow on social media. We could no longer bring him back to rational thinking.

It took so long for our son to come back to reality. At first, we thought the psychiatrists were being too harsh when they started talking about bipolar disorder. We thought things would just pass. But as the days went on and he was still in a different world, we started to understand this was a new journey. It was painful to watch his brain being possessed by "someone else." The things he believed, felt, and perceived were so different from who he was and from reality. He thought everyone, including us and the medical staff, were all playing a charade, trying to fool him. He went from lying on the floor crying in a fetal position to jumping up and down in bursts of joy. He was anxious, upset, angry, and hyper, as he experienced a wide range of emotions.

You feel so helpless as a parent trying to get your kid "back," trying to make his thoughts return to some sense of normalcy, but you must wait. They tried different medications, different dosages, and different combinations, and all of them had some side effects—drowsiness, constant hunger, drooling, stuffy nose, and a Parkinson's-like gait.

One of the conditions for his release was the ability to differentiate between delusions and reality. It took nearly two months of trying different medications and adjusting doses before we started to gradually see his old self come back, and he could finally be released. We got a month's supply of medications and flew back home.

While he was in the hospital, we started to research programs, psychiatrists, and therapies for when we got home. We knew this was going to be a long journey. Some of the program staff we talked to said they could handle the mental health side, but not if there had been marijuana use. Others said they could not handle the mental health side. In others, he had to be interviewed, and his answers during the intake process did not convince them he wanted to be helped, so he was not admitted.

He was still fragile, and only a few days after we got back, he started to become anxious again, and he believed that certain everyday things had meaning, like seeing someone with a certain hat or a certain show on television. He needed further professional psychiatric help.

We arrived at the local emergency department in the morning and were taken to a special observation unit. A psychiatrist saw him in the evening and reassessed his condition, and he was admitted around midnight. Since he was 18, he had to be escorted by security personnel to the adult mental health unit of the hospital, and I could not accompany him anymore. The scenes from that day were unreal, like it was happening to someone else. It was like we were on a hamster wheel, and we were unable to get off.

He still has horrible memories of the time spent there. Even though he was still not completely mentally back, he remembers, and he can't even talk today about some of the events of that stay. Some adults were screaming, some talking in gibberish, some walking with their shorts halfway down, and at one point, someone got so aggressive the police had to be called and visitors were asked to leave—but my kid had to stay behind.

This experience was yet another terrible waiting game—trying to get the right medications and combinations of medications until the psychiatrist on call could determine if he was ready to leave. Except for a few days when we got home, he had spent over three months in mental health hospitals since his first episode.

He was finally released to us. Next, he had to attend an intense six-hour-a-day outpatient program. He learned different coping techniques and skills from dialectical behavior therapy (DBT). After six weeks, he was enrolled in a reduced program for three hours a day.

He was now reaching a period of stability and awareness with lots of walks and time spent together. The medications were continually being fine-tuned, and he was back with us.

He said he wanted to try to go to college. He had been admitted, after all. So, a semester after he was supposed to start, he enrolled in his classes.

He went to college for a couple of semesters. It was tough letting him go, but we did not want to squash his dreams. We wanted to show him we trusted him, believed in him, and wanted him to live through this college experience. He met a lot of good friends who helped support him.

He did well the first semester. We picked him up from college every weekend so he could attend weekly counselor visits, and so we could check in.

The second semester was different, though. The availability of marijuana and friends using was too much of a temptation. At this point he thought, *Lesson learned. I just won't use anything too strong. It just happened once.* He believed he could medicate his anxiety by smoking marijuana.

Unfortunately, his brain reacted almost immediately. He rapidly spiraled again into a state of hyperactivity and hypersensitivity. He lost his appetite, felt tremendous anxiety, and couldn't sleep. He distanced himself from us, though he had an internal radar or compass that let him know he was off course, and he asked us for help. He was very distraught.

His psychiatrist sent us to the emergency department at another hospital so our son could be assessed. After a long day of tests and waiting, he was sent to another medical clinic. At least this time we felt the experience would not be as traumatic because it was a smaller center. This time, we could not visit because of COVID. He was released after 10 days, and again, he started back on medications and counseling.

We had a brief period of stability, but some of his anger and anxiety still lingered. His emotions were raw and intense. He was in a constant state of "fight, flight, or freeze," and he decided the only way to change things was to leave. He cut ties with his counselors and therapists, his friends, family, social media, and the one passion he loved—his music. Music was a passion that made him feel creative but also very stressed. He was very resourceful as a musician, and we were impressed with the things he accomplished, but the demands in the music industry are huge, and the negative feedback from social media platforms just crushed him.

He met a wonderful girl at college who was an amazing, healthy, and caring influence. They decided to leave together to find a place where they could live away from the triggers and memories.

It was not an easy time. He stopped communicating with us, and we were afraid he would spiral down into another episode if things got tough. We told his girlfriend that if our help was ever needed, we would be there.

They found a place to live; they got away from a lot of triggers and memories, and he gradually started communicating with us. They started fresh. He made commitments to his girlfriend and himself, and he has not smoked marijuana since. He stopped taking medication.

Several years on this plan has worked. My son is stable today. He is in a loving relationship, and we have a relationship with him as well, which is one of the things I treasure the most—the ability to communicate, know how he is doing, and just tell him we love him.

I would never take this season of goodness for granted. I know some things are still fragile. He has decided to no longer take medication. He still has lots of anxiety and a tendency to dwell on negative thoughts.

There are scars. There are awful memories. There is his unwillingness to talk about this period, though he now and again mentions some things about the past, with lots of shame. We do not push, though. We encourage him to focus on today. We try to listen more, and we try to avoid fixing everything. We let him know how proud we are. He makes his medical decisions, and we can only suggest and provide support.

Today, I am just grateful for his mental health stability and the fact he is alive and got out of the spiral of addiction. I count each new day as a gift. We are not naïve as to what could happen. We no longer feel like we're walking on eggshells or jumping every time the phone rings. It was a bad period, but he emerged. He did the work. He made drastic decisions at a young age. He had to make tough choices. He has become a young adult.

Even though we went with our children to almost every school presentation and educational session on the dangers of drug use (some of them led by very emotional, grieving parents, and others by kids, revealing their creativity in how they concealed their habits and use), these messages didn't land with our son. Even though kids know the use of concentrates and dabbing can interfere with their brains the way it did with our son, many will not think twice about using them. They don't accept there is the potential of losing their mind, not knowing if they will get it back, or spending time in a traumatic environment. These are the real consequences of marijuana use our youth don't know a lot about. Or they dismiss these risks by thinking they happen only to people who are already susceptible.

In hindsight, I know there are things I would have done differently. We were clueless as to the strength of the products he was able to get and use.

We were also not strong enough about the consequences outlined in the family contracts we signed with him. It was easier to try to keep the "peace," but the peace never lasted for long.

Our family is lucky. I feel grateful every day for this chance, knowing things could have been very different if our son had not made tough choices and decided to make drastic changes.

CHAPTER 3:

The Unseen Side of Cannabis: A Family's Battle with Psychosis

"CANNABIS-INDUCED PSYCHOSIS? What's that?" I remember asking the doctor this when I took our son into the emergency department (ED) in December 2014. I had never heard of it.

"The only thing showing up in his blood work is THC," the doctor explained. Our long saga apparently had begun years earlier in 2011, unbeknownst to us, when our son started to smoke weed with his high school friends. There was a group that always hung out at the same friend's house. As much as I tried to have our son's "best friend" over to our house, he was never able to come over, or never wanted to, or our son didn't want him at our home. Our son was very smart, funny, witty, and had lots of friends. He was very popular and full of shenanigans to make others laugh. He was kind, very sensitive, and a communicant at our church. He is the youngest of our four children. Our son played high school football, which he had loved since elementary school until he suddenly became disinterested during his senior year of high school. It was such a change for him, but he claimed he was tired of it and gave up trying. He graduated from high school, started college, and decided to rush a fraternity in the second semester of his freshman year. He was excited to join the fraternity. That summer, he did poorly at his job.

First Psychotic Break

In fall 2013, he was back at college for his sophomore year and initiation into the fraternity, which meant *a lot of hazing*. It was out of control. The fraternity was nothing like the sororities I had known in my college days, where an adult house mother lived in the sorority house. These young men were unsupervised with no limits as to how far the hazing could go. I remember our son calling me one night complaining how terrible it was, and I told him he didn't need to go through with it. He said he had come this far and didn't want to quit after all he had already gone through. He said the fraternity would always be there for him and thought it would look good on his résumé. I told him my sorority contacts never helped further my career. He was initiated into the fraternity and came home for Thanksgiving.

During his second semester, we received several unusual phone calls from him. I was confused as his speech was perfectly normal, but what he was saying was nonsensical. He would very seriously tell me about our name and its meaning with numbers and explain this was how he connected with others. There were a lot of religiosities as well. He traced our family tree, he claimed, back to kings and queens. He completed his sophomore year, but his grades had fallen since his freshman year.

We all drove out for his sibling's graduation in May 2014. On our way, our son suddenly, halfheartedly, tried to jump out of our moving car. When we returned home, we took him to a psychiatrist who prescribed an anti-depressant. That July, he was to study abroad. The morning he was to leave, he was sobbing, not wanting to go. We convinced him it would be hard to cancel, and it could be good for him. He had started the antidepressant just two weeks before, so we hoped things would improve for him. With mixed emotions, we put him on the flight. He ended up having a great time, and the antidepressant seemed to help him. However, a month after returning, he discontinued the antidepressant and started smoking weed. He returned to college for the fall semester of his junior year, and things really went downhill.

Two weeks after Thanksgiving, his roommate called us to say he was acting strangely but couldn't really explain what was going on. I immediately drove up to the university and found him walking around the apartment with a large walking stick, banging the floor. He was paranoid, crying, and not himself at all. His roommates said he had been smoking a lot of weed. It was finals week, and he had no idea he had already missed several of his final exams! Somehow, I convinced him to come home with me and go straight to the ED. He ended up in the psychiatric unit, and 48 hours later, they discharged him. To our complete surprise and dismay, he was diagnosed with cannabis-induced psychosis (CIP). We had never heard of it. I can't describe the intense worry I experienced, wondering if our son would ever return to himself. We walked on eggshells constantly. He was given an antipsychotic and an anti-anxiety medication. Two weeks later, the day before Christmas Eve, we took him back to the hospital after we witnessed him waving a large kitchen knife around and then climbing a tree in his bathrobe while waving a wooden samurai sword. We told the ED personnel his history and pleaded with them to keep him longer and figure out what was wrong. They promised they would, but 72 hours later, to our profound disbelief, he was discharged once again.

His friends were adamant there was no way weed could be the cause of his issues. We withdrew him from classes for the next semester and had his previous semester classes withdrawn because his grades had been so poor. He stayed home the next semester, was miserable, and saw a psychiatrist every couple of weeks. There were many medication changes over the next few months. He couldn't sleep at all, and then he slept a lot. He tried yoga.

One day he sat by himself in my car with the garage door closed and started the engine. Thankfully, I found him right away.

More medication adjustments followed. By summer 2015, he was doing better and started an internship. That fall, he commuted back and forth to college. We became hopeful. He moved into an off-campus apartment to complete his final semester and graduated from college in June 2016. He took a job that summer working at an insurance company.

Second Psychotic Break

He was doing well until he started smoking weed again on April 20, 2017, "420 Day." I had no idea what 420 Day meant. By September 2017, he was fired from his job. That fall he blew up at us for tossing out any weed we found. I was scared, angry, immensely worried, and could not stop crying or praying. After seeing my doctor, I started therapy and began taking an antidepressant.

Then our son decided he was leaving to drive out West to get away from us. My heart was broken. He packed up his car with all his belongings and began his trip. We could see from his bank account how many times he bought weed. It was apparent he was smoking it while driving, based on his posting of strange videos on social media. He ended up in Washington state and spent many nights in his car. He found an apartment there and smoked weed all day, every day. He had plenty of money from his previous jobs, so he was financially independent.

By February 2018, we noticed his inappropriate posts on social media, and we reported him. He was kicked off Facebook. He was clearly psychotic, smoking weed constantly, eating edibles, and drinking a lot of wine. He became so psychotic my husband and older son flew out to try to get help. We notified the police of what was happening, and they assured us they would help. During their wellness check, our son came out wielding a knife, which, thankfully, he dropped. They quickly realized he was not in his right mind and had EMS transfer him to a local hospital. From there, he was sent to a psychiatric hospital and treated with antipsychotic medication for a new diagnosis of bipolar I disorder.

A month later, my older son and I flew out to pick him up and fly with him to a dual diagnosis residential program, where he would receive inpatient treatment for 45 days. At this point, he was out of psychosis and made great strides while there.

In April 2018, he transitioned to an intensive outpatient program (IOP) in California for several months, and then to a sober living house, where he met a nice young man struggling with alcohol issues. After almost a year, they moved into an apartment together. He had a great couple of years and was back to himself. He started driving for Lyft and started an internship with a new company. Things went well until his roommate decided to move out to live with his girlfriend. A new roommate, who was a very bad influence, moved in and convinced our son to start using kratom, an herbal substance that can produce opioid- and stimulant-like effects.

Third Psychotic Break

Over the next year, he gradually weaned off most of his medications. His new psychiatrist reluctantly started him on a mood stabilizer, and with some reluctance, added an antidepressant. That was a calculated risk since antidepressants can trigger mania. But it ended up being a game changer as he felt so much better. However, in October 2019, he had trouble refilling his prescription for his mood stabilizer due to an issue with his insurance. Two weeks later, it was finally straightened out, but his psychiatrist said she would not renew it since he had already been off it for two weeks.

Around the time he was put on these medications, our son developed severe back acne he had never had before. It was a problem that bothered him, though we had been assured by his doctor the medication and the acne were entirely unrelated. Also, our son's liver enzymes became elevated.

The condition was serious enough that a few months earlier, he had a liver biopsy. During that procedure, he flatlined and had to be seen by a cardiac team. As with the back acne, his liver enzymes returned to normal after he stopped taking the mood stabilizer. These events didn't help his trust in the medical field or of psychiatric medications.

We had a nice, normal Christmas when he came home to visit, and all seemed well. However, one day in January 2020, he left work early to climb up a mountain and had to be rescued by helicopter off the top as he was unprepared for the weather and was lost with night falling quickly. He had been off the mood stabilizer but was still on a high dose of the antidepressant, and possibly kratom. He went into psychosis again but refused any new medications or to see a doctor. He told us he had *not* smoked any weed.

He began to cut back on the antidepressant slowly, and within six months, was back to himself. Unfortunately, at the end of August 2020, he was fired from his job. Apparently, brain scans and imaging done in August 2018 led his psychiatrist to believe he did not have bipolar disorder, so we did not have the ability to protect his employment through a disability claim.

One thing I noticed during those six months when he was in CIP was how many times he would tweet in a day. At the height of his psychosis, he was tweeting 40-plus times a day. As he gradually came out of it, his strange tweets would lessen until, eventually, he stopped tweeting. Monitoring his tweets was helpful for us because we could gauge how he was doing, even when he would try to talk his way around any suspicions we had regarding his state of mind.

Fourth and Hopefully Final Psychotic Break

In October 2020, I called our son and told him how much we missed him and wished he would come back home. He agreed it would be nice as he had no job other than driving for Lyft. So, later that month, I flew out to California and helped him pack up, and we spent two weeks driving his car and belongings back to the Midwest, taking in 10 national parks along the way! It was an amazing trip, and we both loved it. Our son was back to himself!

He moved back into our home, and it was wonderful to have him back. We discussed many things and ideas for his future. He decided he really wanted to go back to college and earn a second degree, a BS in electrical and computer engineering. He applied to several schools and accepted an offer close to our home. He began his engineering degree in the fall of 2021, moved into his own apartment, and attended classes for four consecutive semesters through the fall of 2022.

He said it was on 420 Day in 2022 when he smoked weed again, enticed by all the billboard advertisements. He was 28 now and thought that because his brain was fully developed, it would be okay. It wasn't until February 2023 when things started to unravel again, and we knew we had a problem. He was smoking, using edibles, and vaping high-potency THC products daily. His grades plummeted in college. By May 2023 he was going into CIP, and there was no turning back or talking him out of it.

I tried to engage him in more positive activities, like playing tennis and walking with him, but he kept using THC. I told him how there was research showing weed can lead to schizophrenia, but nothing deterred him. The police did a wellness check on him after someone called about some tweets he had posted. The police talked to him and then left, saying he was friendly, and they had struck up a nice conversation with him. We knew taking him to the hospital was fruitless.

The week of July 4th, while we were returning home from visiting family, our son sent us a text saying my husband's Tesla was now his, or we could pay him $500,000 for it. With the Tesla tracking we could see where he was headed. We were sick. We had always talked about our trip visiting national parks and how fun it would be to have a bucket list to see them all. He was heading to another national park. It wasn't a straight trip as he bought weed numerous times along the way.

We decided to contact our local police and tell them he had "stolen" our car. They assured us they could have him pulled over, charged, and returned to our town with the car. However, when the police arrived to take our report, they said it was not really a "stolen" vehicle, but rather a "joyride" since he had a key and had permission in the past to borrow it. We explained he was driving high and endangering others, and we knew *exactly* where he was at any given moment. They said there was nothing they could do until he returned to our area.

We tracked him traveling through Wisconsin and Minnesota. We thought, *Good, recreational marijuana is illegal in those states.* (It was at that time.) *So maybe he is trying to quit.* But upon checking his bank account, we quickly realized he had gone to several marijuana dispensaries in both states! How could that be? I got on the phone with the state police in Minnesota, who said the 2018 Farm Bill provided a loophole to use hemp to make high-potency THC products. I was furious.

After blowing out a tire and threatening some campers who called the police on him, our son did end up at the national park. He was out of his mind. A week later, he returned home to his apartment. In the meantime, we had gone to the courthouse to get emergency guardianship. So, when he returned, the police were notified and immediately went over to apprehend him. He spent a night in jail but was transferred the next day to a psychiatric hospital, where he stayed for three weeks and was put on antipsychotic medication. When he was somewhat stabilized, we had an interventionist transfer him for a month-long inpatient stay. He improved steadily, and for the first time, apologized and thanked us for getting him out of psychosis. He admitted he could never use weed again. This was a monumental step!

His physicians diagnosed our son again with bipolar disorder, but he had gone several years with no problems, so I remain skeptical of the diagnosis as this could all possibly be CIP. From there, he went to another intensive outpatient program, but the people there were all much younger than him, and he had already gone through so many of the same programs before.

In December 2023, we made the decision to bring him back home. As I write this, it's been six months since our son stopped using THC products on August 7, 2023. Like before, he claims part of his memory and ability to learn have been diminished. He no longer has any friends. We were worried it would be too soon to restart his engineering classes, but he really wanted to return in January 2024. The deep depression following his CIP has been hard on him, but he is trying. He is slowly getting better after starting ketamine treatments under the care of his physician. We are hopeful and continually pray for him, our entire family, and all those whose loved ones have been affected by CIP and cannabinoid hyperemesis syndrome (CHS).

We still have so many questions and concerns and a lot of worries. I'm hopeful as he seems to now understand he can never use THC again. We talk more openly with him now but still feel the eggshells under our feet. Back in 2020, sometime in the middle of all of this, I am thankful I found Johnny's Ambassadors. To this day, I have no recollection of how I found them, but I am so grateful God led me to where I needed to search. I quickly realized we were not alone in this heartbreak and struggle. I started to read the many stories of others who were going through some of the very same symptoms of THC use. When our local police said there was no way THC could do this to our son, I was emboldened to tell them how misinformed they were. I gave them the book *Tell Your Children* by Alex Berenson, along with paper printouts from Johnny's Ambassadors.

I'm realizing more and more how awful this poison is for so many, even though others can apparently be unscathed by it. Time will tell if our son truly has bipolar disorder or not. I believe it will take several more years to figure that out. I am grateful our son knows we love him dearly. Since his apologies, I'm thankful his siblings are there for him and support him. I often question why the medical doctors, who say they see this all the time, aren't speaking up more loudly about these harms. The word is getting out, but the message is hard for so many to hear, because they have been told THC is "natural" and "just a plant." I had an addiction therapist tell me weed is the one drug people will defend to the end of the earth. Unlike any other drug, people insist it is not a problem. I believe that the personal accounts, the research, the violent acts involving THC, and the numbers of people negatively affected tell a very different story.

CHAPTER 4:

Witchcraft

OUR SON WAS A TOP NATIONAL D1 recruit. He broke his leg in November of his senior year and self-medicated with THC vape cartridges to deal with his pain and depression. On the evening of Monday, February 28, our lives changed forever.

It was 7 p.m., and my wife and I were at a high school athletic banquet, waiting for our son to arrive. Our son's varsity team won its first-ever high school sectional championship, thanks in large part to our son. We sat alone and dumbfounded, wondering what was going on, when our son, the team's best player, never showed up.

"Where is your son?" the coach asked.

"No idea. I'm sorry," I said. Parents asked as well with confused expressions. Our family crisis was playing out in public.

My wife phoned him to find out when he was getting there. He replied in a whisper, "I will be there later. I have to see someone. I have to see a girl." We kept calling and texting him. He'd say, "I'll be there soon."

I told him, "If this is about a girl, just see her after the banquet, buddy!" He had only recently gotten involved with girls, and I figured maybe this girl, or his emotions, had gotten the better of him. He stopped responding at about 8:30 p.m. and missed the banquet.

He had been acting strangely leading up to that weekend before the banquet. Friday, when he came home from school, he left a THC vape cartridge on the kitchen counter next to his keys. He said it was an old one, and he found it in the back pocket of the seat of the car. I had recently cleaned out the car searching for paraphernalia, so I called BS, and for the first time, said I was sick and tired of his addiction. An hour later he texted me, "I'm sorry."

Then later that weekend, I found knives in his bedroom and noticed cut marks on his biceps. He also had developed a stress-induced rash over much of his chest, neck, and arms, which we related to his manic state that weekend. On Sunday evening, we had a volatile argument that wasn't good for anyone.

When he did not show up at the banquet, we sensed something was very off. We had been increasingly catching him vaping a particularly popular brand of high-potency THC cartridges. We noticed increasingly strange behavior and an increasing amount of time spent in the bathroom or isolated in his bedroom.

We checked the Life360 app, and his big brother and I headed out searching for him, without any luck. As midnight approached, my wife grew frantic and started texting his teammates to see if they knew where he was, but no one did. Our panic grew as the dreadful thought surfaced that maybe he had hanged himself in a nearby construction site.

At about 1 a.m. we got a call from a police officer, telling us he had picked up our son.

He was alive.

The officer said either he could arrest our son, or we could come pick him up at the high school. When we arrived at the school, the officer told us he picked up our son after he had been on someone's roof and jumping fences. The officer then noted our son said a girl from his class put a "curse on him," and she was into "witchcraft." Then came, "I think your son needs some psychiatric help."

What was going on with my little buddy?

Our son was let out of the car, and he walked bare-chested toward me. I was just happy to see our son alive after fearing the worst. I gave him my down jacket and helped him into the back seat of our car. I did not realize until I found a pile of wet clothes near the washer that evening and wet shoes in the garage the next morning, he had gone swimming in his clothes in someone's pool in the middle of winter. I had been staring at his face, making sure he was okay, and had not realized he was wet from head to toe.

We got home close to 2 a.m., after searching for his phone and my car keys, which he had lost. I hugged our son, looked him in the eyes in the kitchen, teared up, and told him, "Buddy, I'm worried about you. Are you okay?"

He said, "Yeah, I'm okay, Dad. Are you?"

He wasn't okay and neither was I. I was traumatized. I was hoping it was mushrooms or LSD and would wear off by morning, but it was marijuana, and it never wore off.

Before we separated, he mentioned he did not like a certain boy in his class. He said the boy "smelled like Grandpa" and "had Grandpa's eyes." My dad had been in World War II and was our son's hero. He lived to nearly 95. Our son was given a shell casing from his 21-gun salute at his military funeral, which he kept next to his bedside. In our son's subconscious, Grandpa was present in the spirit world, protecting him from the evil spirit and dark forces that were tormenting him.

I went to bed and woke up at about 3:15 a.m. when I noticed the hall lights were on. I went to the garage, opened the door, and found he had taken our new car, and the garage door was left wide open. I was in a complete adrenaline-fueled panic. What was he doing? I called the police and told them what he had done, so at least if someone reported him in their backyard, the police would know it was him and not shoot him.

My wife called our son and pleaded for him to come home. I merged the call with the police, so the dispatcher could talk to our son. The dispatcher asked our son if he wanted to talk to someone. He replied in a gentle voice, "Yeah, maybe." He knew something was wrong as well. The dispatcher kept talking to him and told him to go home to his mom. He came home about 4 a.m. I later learned he left home again at about 5:45 a.m. and came back at about 7 a.m. He was manic and could not sleep. We were exhausted and did not notice.

A whirlwind of psychosis swept us up that week. Our son ended up being arrested the next evening and spent the night in jail. We learned later that week, in a text from our daughter's friend, that he believed the following things about the girl who he thought was into witchcraft:

- She put a curse on him and possessed his parents and was in their heads. He also believed she had mind control over his parents. *In fact, he repeatedly stated he had to kill the 70 percent of his mom that was possessed!*
- She made a man try to molest him in jail.
- She is inside his head and has made him feel suicidal and has forced him to put sharp objects on his arm.
- She "has his ears," like she can hear what he hears.
- She puts him in instant burning or itching pain as soon as he thinks or does something she would not like.
- She is somehow inside the house. She told him to leave the doors unlocked while no one was home, so she could come walk around and do stuff.
- She changes the words he uses in his head.

She forced him to screenshot hundreds of articles about witchcraft.

He thought he had sold his soul to the devil. Luckily, in his darkest hour, he reached out to God and saved an image of Saint Michael stabbing a spear into the devil as a screensaver. This simple act by a scared and tormented teenage boy saved his life. He also believed he swapped souls with a friend at a party. Clearly, he was not well.

The cops visited our house on a wellness check midweek. By the end of the week, I had to call the police on our son to get him psychiatric help. That was the hardest thing I had ever done. I will never forget the image of him crying in the kitchen while FaceTiming his sister, who was away at college. He was pleading not to have us call the police. It was like a horror movie.

After five days in the hospital, he attended five weeks of an intensive outpatient program (IOP) and partial hospitalization program (PHP). The programs offered very little other than teaching him some coping skills. He tested positive for THC during the last week of the program.

He never went back to campus but managed to graduate from high school and walk at graduation. He strongly resisted, as he had so much social fear and shame, but we insisted and told him not to have any regrets. He slayed that dragon and was smiling with joy at graduation.

The Girl and Omaha Beach

We did all we could to nurture our son back. We went fishing, camping, horseback riding, and bike riding, and took many evening walks with the dog. We even slept with him at times. He started school and got back into his sport at junior college with hopes of transferring to a four-year college. He just could not remain sober for longer than about 30 to 35 days.

On Friday, January 20, 2023, I found a half-smoked joint in his jacket. He was going to sleep in and skip his first spring practice due to a "headache," but obviously it was because he got high. He and I argued, and his relapse ruined my birthday weekend. He began acting strangely by Tuesday, exhibiting rapid manic speech and behavior. He had been getting high and spitting his medicine out when we weren't looking. Things were beginning to unravel.

The following Thursday morning, I found him asleep on the bathroom floor with the dog. He told my wife the dog had died and come back to life. By noon he was worse and was staring at his mom and me with an evil glare. My wife and I whispered how we were going to have to hide the knives again for his and our safety. We slept with the bedroom doors locked. We were afraid of our son. This was our reality.

Thursday afternoon he was going to drive to his sports leadership class, but I found him standing in the pantry area and said, "Hey, buddy, I don't think you're in any shape to drive," and he seemed to agree and simply handed me the keys.

He went to the couch to sit down with his elbows on his knees, and his head resting in his hands. He either had too many thoughts going on in his head or was hearing voices. I told him he needed to take his medicine and stay sober, and he told me to be quiet. I now feared he was hearing voices. My wife checked on him 15 minutes later, and he responded with, "Get the f**k out of here."

That evening, his eyes were again demonic as he stared at us. I warned him I would call the police, and he sprinted out of the house. He went for a long walk on the trails in the parkway surrounding our neighborhood and ended up on a hill behind some houses. We tracked him, and at about 10 p.m., we drove over to try to pick him up. His mom called and said she was worried about him, and he said he had to meet some people. She pleaded with him to come to the car. About two minutes later, he knocked on my window and startled me, and I got out of the car.

"Hey, buddy, how are you doing?" I asked. He looked out of his mind.

"I'm okay, Dad. I'm just waiting for somebody." He then asked if it would be okay if a girl could come to our house.

"Sure. Where is she?"

"She is standing right here." There was no one there but our son.

"I'm sorry, buddy. You can see her, but I can't. Which side is she on—the left or the right?"

"She's just here, Dad."

"Well … it's very nice to meet you," I said. "Our son has mentioned a lot of good things about you. We would love to have you over to our house."

I invited our son and his imaginary friend into the car, and my wife drove us home in 10 minutes of utter silence. We knew the next morning we had to take him to the hospital.

That night we decided to have him sleep with his mom and the dog in the master bedroom. I slept on a mattress, blocking the master bedroom door so he could not get out. At 1 a.m. my wife caught him vaping in the bathroom and took it away.

On Friday, January 27, our son walked into our bedroom and declared, "Let's watch Omaha Beach!" He started blaring *Saving Private Ryan* on the TV. I told him he needed help. He and I started arguing and wrestling for my phone when I tried to sneak a video of him. At one point, he locked his mom in our bedroom and raged demonically at her, saying he controlled her. He shoved her on the bed and was screaming at her. Luckily, we had called the police, and they were in the house and heard everything.

We unlocked the door, and my wife ran crying into my arms. The officer got him to agree to a voluntary admittance at the local hospital. This time he was hospitalized for 10 days and released on Monday, February 6. I later found images of a screaming soldier from the "Omaha Beach" scene saved on his phone.

The Plan

Rather than go with us upon discharge from the treatment center, he told us he had his "own plan." I told him he had a bad plan, but I would respect it because he was now 19. We were enforcing boundaries. He could not come home. He hoped to stay with teammates, but he did not realize how sick he was, and we had told everyone not to take him in.

We told him we loved him unconditionally but only supported him in a life of recovery, and we left him behind, driving five hours down the coast to attend my board meeting. We decided we could feel lousy sitting on our couch at home, or we could feel lousy at the beach.

As we pulled into the hotel, our son's teammate texted us that he was with him at In-N-Out Burger and thought he needed professional help. He also said our son wanted to buy marijuana. He dropped him off at a good family friend's house, where he stayed until Wednesday evening, when he had to leave because he was smoking again and psychotic. He tried another neighbor, where he showered and ate a pizza, but left there as well when we suggested she say she was going to take him to the hospital. He then went to another friend's house, but this kid had just come back from nine months of marijuana rehab, and the dad would not allow it. What are the odds?

He texted me at about 11:30 p.m. and said he was ready to go to rehab but just wanted one more night under our roof, and he would leave in the morning. He also texted our daughter's friend that this was his last night of smoking, and he was ready to go to rehab.

He called me pleading to come in from the cold. We said we could leave immediately for rehab, but if not, there was a sleeping bag for him on the front porch. I peered through the blinds at him on our front porch. It tore at my heart. I love this kid so much. I was dying inside but knew this was what had to happen.

He got angry and called the police to get his stuff. The police called and asked what was up, and I explained the situation and how we were trying to get him down to rehab. The officer negotiated with our son, and he agreed to either gather his items and leave or leave immediately for rehab. We agreed at 12:10 a.m. to leave for rehab and left at about 12:31 a.m. for the long drive from Northern California to Los Angeles.

We were 15 minutes down the highway when he rolled down the window and got high in the car! He put on some very cool wraparound shades and smiled a shit-eating grin as I looked at him in the mirror.

"Are you seriously vaping THC in the car?" I barked. No reply. Just a grin. Apparently, this was his last hurrah.

I tried to get the vape cartridge from him, but he freaked, and my wife said to leave him alone, so I pulled over on the freeway. Out of the blue, two California Highway Patrol officers pulled up behind me. Again, we're in a movie! I explained the situation and how we were trying to get him to rehab, and one officer shared that his older brother was also addicted to drugs. He said to drive safely and take care of our son. Meanwhile, my wife convinced him to give her his vape so he wouldn't get arrested.

I exited off Highway I-5 into a Holiday Inn parking lot at 2:10 a.m. We attempted to sleep a bit in our car. At about 2:40 a.m. our son woke up and bolted out of the car. I confronted him to get him back in the car. He shoved me in the chest and yelled, "Let's check into the hotel!"

My quick-thinking wife told him the hotel was full and to get back in the car. It was freezing outside, and I got chills as we got back in the car and drove down the road.

At about 4 a.m., he opened the door of the vehicle as I was driving 75 miles per hour down I-5. We screamed, "Close the door!" In his delusional state, he easily could have "stepped" out of the vehicle and tumbled onto the highway. He closed the door and went back to sleep. Like we didn't have enough going on!

I took another power nap at 5 a.m. while my wife drove. She does not have great nighttime vision and some fog had settled in on the highway, so I slept with one eye open. I dozed off for maybe 30 minutes. At about 5:50 a.m., the owner of the rehab replied to my text, alerting his team they had an "incoming." We were not even sure whether they could take him in that state.

My wife drove for an hour until we got gas and used the restroom. All the time, we were rushing and just praying he would not wake up. Thankfully, he did not, and I took over driving. At about 9 a.m. we switched drivers again. I took another 15-minute power nap.

We drove all night and arrived at 9:35 a.m. on Thursday, February 9, 2023. He was still sleeping in the back seat. When he got out of the car, he threw water in his mom's face. I motioned to her with my face not to react. We did it. The plan worked.

He was still psychotic, though, and seeing evil spirits in his residential living house. On Monday, he wanted to leave the program. He was determined, so we arranged a companion service to stay with him in a hotel for two days until he returned. On the second evening, he bolted to the Hyatt lobby, paranoid of his companion and thinking his MP3 player was tapped. Rather than go back to his hotel room, he wanted to go with the paramedics to the hospital to get "cleared" to return to rehab the next day. Unfortunately, he was then hospitalized for another week in LA. Thankfully, he advocated for himself to get back to the rehab and coordinated his own return.

That started a very long process of medical treatment, private and group therapy, self and family healing, sobriety skills training, and making new friendships in recovery. He attends several weekly support meetings, goes to school part-time, and works part-time.

On November 12, 2023, he shared his story as he was baptized. On February 10, 2024, he celebrated one year of sobriety. In the summer of 2024, he hopes to start working part-time at the rehab program. He wants to study psychology and work in the mental health field, helping people with substance abuse issues.

This never should have happened. Our son is a victim of an unsafe consumer product. However, God has a plan for him. Don't quit before a miracle happens!

CHAPTER 5:
Blindsided

"A PARENT'S WORST NIGHTMARE" is an understatement. Never in my life would I have imagined I would be walking down this nightmare of a journey of the past three and a half years with my son, John. They say God gave mothers an inner strength to endure childbirth and a hardness that allows them to take care of their families through sickness and fatigue without fail. The journey I am navigating today breaks me into tiny pieces every single day. A child never stops being your child, and when they break, you break with them. But somehow, with my faith in God and support from my closest girlfriends, my chosen family, and my courageously strong daughter, I have found the strength to keep going and *not* give up.

I feel it's important to share my views on marijuana and give full transparency prior to my son's crisis with THC. In late high school, throughout my college years, and even into young adulthood before marriage, I drank alcohol and dabbled with smoking marijuana on occasion. I am Generation X and never considered myself "anti-weed." We "worked hard and partied hard," but if we were achieving our goals in life, it all seemed so harmless.

Sadly, the weed of today is not the weed of our fathers or even like the weed from 30 years ago, for that matter. It is more potent than ever before, and with vapes, edibles, dabs … you name it … our society is consuming cannabinoids at an incredible rate. And, unfortunately, with legalization and increased access to these high-potency THC products, our youth are at more risk than ever before.

Please don't be naive like me and think, *It's just a little pot. Nothing bad will happen*, or *They're just being teenagers.* Today, I share John's story so parents realize this crisis is real, this can happen to their child, and it is preventable. I hope by sharing my story, it will help other parents recognize the signs of THC addiction, understand the horrible consequences that can happen with cannabis-induced psychosis (CIP), and intervene way earlier than I did with my son.

I was married for 13 years and had two children—my son, John, and then my daughter. My ex-husband was diagnosed with bipolar (BP) disorder several years after we were married, and he continued to drink excessively throughout our marriage. John's struggle was not my first experience with mental health and addiction issues. John was extremely intelligent, enjoyed wrestling and football, and had a great group of friends. John was so smart he tested "off the charts" but also seemed bored and unfocused at school. He was diagnosed with ADHD around fourth grade, which was also around the time I was going through my divorce.

Once John got to high school, he seemed to outgrow his ADHD and his need for medication. But in the back of my mind, I always knew there was a chance John had a predisposition to bipolar disorder. I thought everything with John was "normal," and then the COVID lockdowns happened. It was isolation, social media, and nonstop video gaming. Little did I know at the time, but this is when John started vaping THC, at age 16. The summer of John's junior year, he was on his way to work early in the morning and crashed into a telephone pole, totaling his car. He blamed it on the wet road conditions. The police officer said, "I've never seen a car so wrecked where the driver walked away without a scratch." John was higher than a kite from THC that morning, and he's lucky he didn't kill himself or someone else.

His senior year in high school, John opted to stay at home and finish school virtually. I had no idea he was vaping THC during the day in my home that last year, let alone for over two years. Somehow, John successfully graduated from high school and was accepted to college into an engineering program.

The summer before college, John wrecked and totaled his second car, driving like a maniac on a curvy road late at night. He blamed it on a deer jumping in front of him. Again, John was high from THC and probably showed signs of early mania from BP disorder, but I didn't know that then either.

John started college in the fall of 2021. It was the happiest and proudest moment of my life as a single parent. He was so smart and had his whole life ahead of him to succeed and fulfill his dreams. I wish I had known to ask my son in college if he was using alcohol or marijuana to help him cope with the change and challenges of college life. John was using weed with high amounts of THC to cope, but I thought it was "casual use" and "the thing they do in college."

On Thanksgiving break, John came home very sick. He looked horrible and had a terrible cough. I had to drag him to the doctor, as he didn't want to go and was becoming very aggravated with me. Not only did John have pneumonia, but it was so bad they had to give him breathing treatments in the office. On the drive back to college, I begged John to stop smoking pot and stay focused on his studies. He agreed and promised that after this health scare, he would stop smoking marijuana and do his best to finish his finals and get through his first semester of college.

On December 7, 2021, I received a call from an emergency department (ED) doctor at 4:15 a.m., stating John was brought in by the campus police with mania and psychosis. They explained they had to sedate John to get him stabilized, and he was in transit by ambulance going to a psychiatric hospital in our home city. Here is where my worst nightmare as a single parent began. The surge of emotions I felt that morning—fear, helplessness, and sadness—will forever be etched into my memory. My daughter and I immediately rushed to the hospital to meet the ambulance only to be told John had been taken directly to the inpatient psychiatric unit, and we could not see him. My heart dropped. *How could this be?* I thought. *I am his mother. He needs me. I need to see him. I need to help him!*

After waiting around for hours and repeatedly being told we could not see John, my daughter and I finally went home. I waited for almost 12 hours until the psychiatrist finally called me at 9:40 p.m. that night. The doctor diagnosed John with BP disorder based on John's mania and his dad's history of BP. I was relieved, and I accepted the BP diagnosis, having known this day would likely come. However, what I didn't realize at the time was the mania wasn't solely from underlying bipolar disorder—the high-potency THC had induced major psychosis.

The next day, my daughter and I went to visit John for 30 minutes in the inpatient psychiatric unit. It was like a scene from a movie that cannot be fully described here. John was in full-blown psychosis, not just mania, like I had seen in my ex-husband before. This was different. John was saying he was sent from God to kill the evil people, he had talked to Einstein, and he had enough money to buy the entire planet and the hospital he was in. Terrifying!

Those next eight days and nights were unimaginable and the worst thing I have ever experienced as a mother. It felt like I was blindfolded— you suddenly feel completely powerless, and you have no way of knowing where you are, how you got here, and how you're going to get through the next day. You're blinded and in pain. It's scary when your once loving child no longer acts like himself or sounds sane!

I remember going to John's college dorm room to get all his belongings. There I found a glass bong, two glass bowls, a "one-hitter," dozens of spent vape pens, and a huge bag of pot. I thought to myself, *Was this just high-potency weed? Or was it laced with something?* I remember throwing away all the paraphernalia and weed except a small sample of the "bud," as I wanted to have it analyzed. After eight nights, John finally came home and literally slept for almost two weeks straight. Slowly but surely, he was coming out of psychosis and mania.

During Christmas break, John was adamant about returning to college and felt if he were on medication for his BP, he would be able to thrive and succeed. So, he registered with the Disabilities Office, got a solo dorm room, and returned to college for the spring semester. I wish I had known then what I know now—my son didn't just have bipolar disorder; he had an addiction to high-potency THC products. John barely made it through that semester, as he was not very med-compliant and continued his THC use.

One of the most frustrating things throughout this experience was the lack of knowledge and understanding within the medical community and John's providers about CIP. I just followed along because they were the medical experts. I joined a parent group on Facebook for bipolar disorder support, which led to another group for CIP support. Now I understood the connection and the type of care John needed, but finding it was easier said than done. The next three years were a mind-boggling blur, trying to navigate through John's health condition and addiction to THC. I could literally write an entire book; however, I will walk you through the condensed version.

In the fall of 2022, John transferred to a different college, hoping a change in the environment would be more conducive for him. After two ED visits for depression and suicidal ideation, I found him a new psychiatrist and therapist located on campus. That only took five months, and we were halfway through the school year. I also finally got John to sign legal medical power of attorney forms and to give me access to his health information. John's new psychiatrist diagnosed him with CIP and cannabis use disorder (CUD) on top of the primary bipolar I diagnosis.

Despite my attempts to find John the best providers, he was still in denial, was not very med-compliant, and missed many of his appointments.

John came home on spring break super depressed. He had lost 40 pounds, wasn't eating, was dehydrated, and had not stopped smoking THC. He was a train wreck. I suggested his mental health was most important and encouraged him to withdraw from his classes, but John went back to school anyway. A week later, he called me crying and said he was withdrawing and leaving school. For the next two months, John was severely depressed and slept a lot. He refused to do virtual appointments with his providers or take any medications. Eventually, he started vaping THC behind my back, and the mania started again.

On Memorial Day weekend in 2023, John came home on a Saturday from work in between a double shift. He had a "breakdown" with mania and psychosis again. Hearing voices, talking to himself in the shower, mood swings everywhere, deep sadness, loud laughter, drop-to-the-floor crying, and teeth-grinding rage, along with an hour of psychosis, where "people could hear us." Then he threatened to kill me and "chop me into little pieces," so the police could never find me. Once he left for work again, I immediately called our crisis intervention hotline and spoke with a social worker. We arranged to have the police and the social workers come and get John after he got home from work. John was taken unwillingly to the psychiatric emergency services (PES) unit and then transferred the next day to another inpatient psychiatric unit on a 72-hour involuntary hold.

This time John was angry with me and filled with hatred. Even though I had power of attorney, he wouldn't give me his patient access code. The facility let him out early even though the doctors and director of nursing promised me they were going to get a legal extension on his hold. John showed up at my home unannounced with his father and said, "Thanks for trying to lock me up again. I am moving in with Dad." So, I helped him pack up all his things, and off he went. Sometimes the need for relief beats out the sadness; I needed a break from John and all of it. I felt I had done all I could do for him. So, for the next three months, John was gone from my life, and it was in God's hands. All I could do was pray for him from a distance.

In September 2023, John had somehow managed to enroll in classes at our local college but never made it to class. He was still in psychosis that dated back to the May hospitalization, not taking his medication for his bipolar disorder, and still using THC.

John wasn't getting much supervision or support living at his father's house. One night at 4 a.m., John was high on THC after not sleeping for three days straight and totaled his third car. Once again, he walked away without any injuries, and a random stranger gave him a ride back to his dad's house.

Several days later, John spent an entire day walking around our city in the rain. My daughter and I were concerned, so we found his location on Snapchat and went to pick him up. John was eating at Steak 'n Shake. I walked over to his table, and he said, "Get the hell out and leave me alone, or I'll beat you up." He had his backpack with him, which contained a water bong and had a homemade self-defense stick device with a blade on it. He threatened to use his "weapon" on me, so I immediately went out to my car and called 911.

Once again, the police and the crisis intervention social workers arrived, and John was taken unwillingly to the PES unit. John was admitted to a different psychiatric hospital. This time the medical team was able to break through to him, and John finally admitted he had a problem with marijuana and wanted treatment. John was receptive to having his sister and me visit this time and was remorseful for his actions. He cried, he told us he loved us, and he hugged us for the first time in a very long time. John then spent 11 nights in inpatient care and was transferred to another city for residential dual diagnosis treatment (six weeks) and then partial hospitalization (two weeks).

This facility was in-network for my commercial health insurance and the only thing I could afford for John at the time. It was subpar. The clinicians were not doing what they promised to do for him. He was not getting one-on-one therapy. It was a complete nightmare. However, he was safe, and he was sober from weed for the first time in almost five years.

During John's residential hospitalization, his dad went into rehab for his alcoholism, and then my daughter ended up in the hospital with a nervous breakdown as well. So, my son, my daughter, and my ex-husband were all in the hospital at the same time. This was the hardest heartbreak I've ever felt, and it took everything I had not to fall apart myself.

And to top off an already horrible situation, I had just found out my company was letting go of 200 employees for commercial downsizing. I thought, *Great. Now, that's icing on the cake. I'm losing my job as well.*

How do you put your oxygen mask on first and then help everyone else in this situation? I was drowning and didn't know who to save first. So, I shifted my focus onto my daughter and getting her stabilized to be able to cope with everything that was going on with her dad and her brother first. She came home after six nights, and then we focused on intense therapy.

In early November, John was released early from partial hospitalization because he was not getting the type of care he needed. On the drive home, I made a strict contract with John that I would be drug testing him weekly. If he were going to live with me, there would be no THC use. John happily agreed and swore he would not smoke THC ever again.

For the next two months, everything went great. John was remaining sober and THC-free, and I felt I finally had my sweet, loving, and caring son back. Then at the end of January, John's dad got out of rehab, got two DUIs in 10 days, and went to jail. He was sentenced to six months in jail and seven years of suspended driving privileges, and he lost his job. This hit both of my children hard, but John particularly. John slipped while coping with his dad's situation and started vaping THC again. I begged him to stop as he failed his drug test. He continued to do it in his car and with his friends, but not in my house.

All the experts and the books I have read tell us to stick to our boundaries and kick children out of the house if they won't follow the rules. I am not ready to take this step of kicking John out because bipolar disorder complicates everything. John has nowhere to go, so it would mean being homeless, or living in a shelter, self-medicating with illicit drugs, or even suicide. It's hard for us to send our sick child to his death. We feel like the rest of the world and our friends and family don't understand that, either.

They say you can divorce your spouse, but not your child. And especially not a child who has bipolar disorder, CIP, and CUD. For me, that has been one of the hardest things to come to grips with recently. I spent two years trying to get John into the best psychiatry program offered in my city, and he just had his first appointment two weeks ago. His psychiatrist understands CIP and is getting John connected to an addiction specialist counselor.

I think one of the many challenges of this mental health crisis in dealing with CIP is being labeled and stigmatized as bad parents. We are just people. We are not perfect, and we are supposed to find a way to help them through it, but there are so many challenges and barriers. For me, I will take every hug, every conversation, every moment I can right now with John. At least he is alive. It isn't perfect, and I know this nightmarish journey is far from over, but I am putting faith in the people and programs available to John. Plus, I am still interviewing to find a full-time job, and I don't have the bandwidth or energy in me to make him leave.

I am shifting my focus now from the past three-and-a-half-year nightmare and finally moving from a place of constant anxiety, worry, and fear into a place of knowing. Navigating through bipolar I disorder and CIP is a process and a journey. As they say in recovery circles, "Healing is not linear," which is true for my son, John, my daughter, and me.

I would also like to acknowledge and thank Laura Stack and Johnny's Ambassadors. This group and Laura's support have been a lifeline for me. I don't know where I would be today or if John would be alive without them.

CHAPTER 6:

No One Would Listen

THERE WAS A TIME WHEN I was a different person. A time when I was a mother with a full and happy heart. There was a time when I had three beautiful, happy boys. It was a fun time. As a child, I wanted nothing more than to be a mother. I always felt I would have sons, and I adored being a boy mom. I still adore being a boy mom. Jacob first made me a mom.

Jacob was born in Wisconsin in 2001. He was an incredibly handsome baby with beautiful skin and dark hair. Jacob was also quite the handful—he would *never* stop crying. Doctors called him "colicky." After a rough first year, our little family found our groove. When Jacob was 20 months old, we welcomed his little brother. Life was busy. Life was good.

Our family moved to Virginia when Jacob was three. I was a stay-at-home mom and loved taking them to the beach, the pool, the zoo, the movies, and the aquarium. We were your "average" family. The boys participated in various sports and playdates. We participated in many scouting adventures that involved the whole family. We loved taking road trips. Times were fun, and the boys were easy. I still remember telling someone once I would have seven more like Jacob. He was sensitive, quiet, and obedient. He followed the rules. He did well in school and had many friends. He loved to tell jokes and make us laugh with his sarcastic and goofy sense of humor. When Jacob was 11, we added one more brother to the mix. Jacob was a wonderful big brother to our youngest one.

For many years, I thrived and adored raising our three boys. Things started changing when Jacob turned 16. He could be moody and difficult with one of his brothers. I thought it was just a sibling thing, or possibly a hormonal thing. I would tell him to be nicer and watch his attitude, but he would get upset with me for calling *him* out and never his brother. Despite that behavior, Jacob was still doing well in school. He was still polite to others, but for some reason, he was rude and obnoxious to his brother.

Over time, Jacob became that way to me. I would ask him what the problem was, and he would respond with snarky answers. I didn't understand him. He rarely smiled. He never shared anything with us. He seemed angry. We would try and talk with him but didn't get much in return. I decided to go to his school for help. No one saw it. "What?" they'd say. "Jacob? He's nothing but polite." I brought him in for therapy once, but that didn't progress because Jacob wouldn't share. He would always seem very calm and say everything was fine. Since Jacob and I were arguing more, and he wouldn't accept help by going to a therapist, I went to see a counselor to learn how our family could cope and handle what was happening with Jacob. After a few sessions, the therapist suggested a psychological exam for him. So, we did that. While we waited six weeks for the results, I received a phone call from his school counselor, who shared that Jacob told a friend he was thinking about suicide.

I *immediately* tried to get help. Driving Jacob to a children's mental health facility and trying to have him admitted was, at the time, the hardest thing my husband and I had ever done. I was terrified, but I knew it had to be done. The experience was a total, complete nightmare. Jacob again told the staff there, "Everything is fine." They asked him if he wanted to be there. He said, "No," and that was it. They didn't seem to care or hear our side of

NO ONE WOULD LISTEN

the story, which included texts from the school counselor and his friend stating that Jacob said he was considering suicide. Even though Jacob was still under 18, they just listened to *him*. So, that ended that effort to seek help for Jacob.

We decided to get Jacob back in weekly therapy. After six months, the psychologist told me Jacob just wouldn't share with him. The psychologist told us he normally heard kids complain about their parents all day, but Jacob never once complained about us. I said to the doctor, "Isn't that proof Jacob is lying? I mean, what kid doesn't complain about their parents?" The psychologist offered him medications for his moodiness. Again, even though he was under 18, he got to say no. Mom's voice meant nothing. So, it seemed after two psychological exams, we had no real diagnosis. We all concluded Jacob would hopefully learn what he needed from being out in the world. We never heard about suicide again. Jacob constantly denied having any such thoughts. His grades were good, and he seemed happy with his friends. So, we thought maybe Jacob had worked through those issues. On his 18th birthday, the same week he graduated from high school, Jacob moved out of our house and in with a friend. Fiercely independent and stubborn, we thought maybe now he would be happier, "free" from us.

When Jacob moved out, community college had been the plan, so we were quite surprised when he joined the military instead. In November of 2019, we drove to Great Lakes, Illinois, to watch our boy graduate from boot camp. We were all so proud. While in the military, we kept in touch with weekly phone calls. That Christmas, Jacob came home on leave, and we had a wonderful 10 days together. Things seemed to be going well until April of 2020. That is when I received a phone call from Jacob's military friend, who informed us Jacob had been lying about things going well. Instead, Jacob was apparently having suicidal thoughts again. While talking with the military doctor, Jacob was asked if he ever had those thoughts before. He replied, "Yes." Since Jacob had denied thoughts of suicide on his military application, it was used as grounds for his discharge. Jacob never shared any of this with us. I made numerous phone calls and exchanged emails with the military and others trying to get Jacob medical help *before* they discharged him. I *begged* people to read his very graphic texts, to talk to his friends, and to stop listening to Jacob. No one listened to me. They listened to Jacob.

About one month after his discharge, Jacob showed up on our doorstep. He had been living with his military friend, but it became problematic. Jacob's only interest at that time was to smoke pot all day while his friend was encouraging him to get a job. Not liking being told what to do, Jacob decided to come back to Virginia and live in his car. I offered our home, but he refused. He did come over often, though, when he'd play with his youngest brother, have dinner, or take a shower. He was homeless for about two weeks before he caved and asked to move back in. We talked. We had a plan. He needed to work full-time and save money to get a place. He agreed, saying that was also what he wanted. He did get a full-time job right away and worked very hard. About a month after living with us, I found him smoking pot in our home, and told him if that was how he wanted to live his life, he would have to move out. The discussion was calm and peaceful. He said he would stop. We never smelled it on him again or found him smoking while living in our home. He lived with us for about eight months until he bought his own condo in January of 2021. He was going to live with a friend. He was excited, and we were excited for him. We thought, well, *now* he can finally be truly happy.

Jacob was very proud to buy his own place at the young age of 19. It was fun to see him decorate and find his own style. That would be short-lived. Just five months after moving out, and four days before his 20th birthday, I got a phone call out of the blue from his old military friend. The cops were called to Jacob's condo, and they took him to the hospital. Jacob had been on his deck, waving a machete around, telling his friends his parents were going to kill him. This phone call was a complete shock. Jacob had just spent the afternoon with us a few days prior and everything seemed fine. His friend said Jacob was having extreme paranoia and delusions. As other friends started talking to us, more stories came out. We learned the summer before Jacob joined the military, after he had moved out of our house, these kids were smoking pot all summer and tried LSD. Jacob had told his friend he never felt the same after that summer. During boot camp, he had begun to experience changes in his mind. An entry from his boot camp journal dated October 13, 2019, just weeks after joining the military, read: "The darkness (over my mind) didn't come today. I wonder how long it will be before things change again." Other entries mention "memory loss" and "dissociation." We didn't know it at the time, but the summer of 2019 with his friends had marked the beginning of Jacob's end.

Jacob's psychosis continued. He had been calling our adult friends, trying to get information about a murder he claimed happened while on a scouting trip years ago. Then there was the time Jacob thought we were not really his parents. Instead, we were part of the Mafia that had kidnapped him from Wisconsin. He called my in-laws looking to find the hit man we had used to kill his real parents. At his brother's high school graduation party that summer, he told his friends I was using the caterer to poison him.

While hospitalized that summer, he was diagnosed with psychosis and bipolar disorder. He turned 20 years old in the mental hospital and was there for approximately 10 days. Somehow, in what felt like an instant, we went from a "normal" life to psychosis. How does that happen? Jacob had multiple psychological exams and an extensive physical to get into the military. Nothing was ever found.

The only thing different in Jacob's life was THC. Yes, Jacob had problems, but we never saw even a hint of paranoia or delusions in all the years he lived with us—which was his whole life except for about 18 months. Severe delusions and paranoia started just months after moving into that condo and feeling free to use marijuana again. His roommate told me that things were great in the beginning, but once Jacob started using THC again, he quickly withdrew from friends, stopped sleeping, and became easily agitated.

Now Jacob was sick and alone. Jacob would *never* admit any of this to us and never did. In fact, shortly after his hospitalization, he came over to our house unexpectedly. It was June 30, 2021, and the day is forever etched into my mind. He acted like his old self and like nothing had ever happened. In hindsight, I sometimes wonder if I should have asked him about everything that day. At the time, I wasn't sure what his mental state was. I didn't know if he'd get angry with me and act out. His friend told us we should be worried for our safety as Jacob was angry with us "for killing his real parents," so I didn't know how to handle him in a safe way, especially because he showed up completely unannounced, and had refused to answer any of my texts since he had been hospitalized. So, I just followed Jacob's lead. As we talked, he seemed to be in a decent mood. He helped his littlest brother fix something on his iPad and gave him a hug, telling him he was sorry he hadn't been around lately. Even more poignant, he sought out his other brother just to tell him something. Jacob *never* wanted to see or talk to that brother, so that was instantly very odd to me. Before he left, I asked him for a hug. He gave me one. I told him, "I love you," and he replied, "I love you, too."

None of us ever saw or spoke to Jacob again. He never texted me again. In my heart, I know now this was Jacob saying goodbye. I know he was trying to spare us. Jacob was scared and was afraid of disappointing us, letting us see his troubles and vulnerabilities. I repeatedly texted him during the next months with no answers. I called. No answer. I would drive to his condo to see if his car was there and whether it had been moved. During the late summer months of 2021, we would get word someone heard from him. So that would reassure me, and my anxiety would calm down. But by mid-October, after checking with his friends yet again, and having knocked on his door for weeks with no answer, I realized no one had heard from Jacob in quite a while. I sent Jacob a text, and for the first time ever, it didn't go through. My heart sank. This kid was *all* about electronics, so I knew there was no way he would disconnect his cell phone. I immediately went over knocking on his door again … no answer. The police happened to drive by for a separate incident. I took that as a sign from God to talk to them. I told them Jacob had been previously hospitalized, diagnosed with bipolar disorder, and suicidal. I told them I was worried his text had bounced back, and no one had heard from him.

The cop told me, "He probably just couldn't pay his bill."

I told the cop, "Or he's dead somewhere."

His car was parked right there. The cop told me to stand away as he knocked on his door. No answer. There was nothing more to do but file a missing person report, which we did right there on the sidewalk.

Just a short time later, on November 2, 2021, two homicide detectives knocked on our door to say they found Jacob in his bedroom. Jacob died by suicide and had been dead for many weeks. He had been dead inside his condo all those same weeks I had been knocking. The neighbor who lived below Jacob spotted the flies in the upper window and called the police. Incredibly, I had been there with my youngest son, knocking on the door *the exact same morning*, but we didn't notice those flies high up in the window! In a way, it was a blessing I didn't notice the flies. I don't think I could have handled being there as they broke into his condo and found his body. Going into that condo, seeing, smelling, and cleaning the aftermath was traumatic enough.

Everything went to hell in a very short amount of time. Jacob had been diagnosed with psychosis and bipolar disorder in June of 2021 and was dead by the end of September. Jacob was so loved. He was very smart. We raised him in church. He graduated with honors from high school. He was an Eagle Scout. He was a Veteran. He was our son. He was a brother. He was an uncle. He had many friends. He loved computers and wanted to design video games. He had a good job.

Jacob had a hard time being open and talking about his issues. He tried to self-medicate his issues with THC, and it opened a world of hallucinations, delusions, and paranoia. Jacob was strong and had the strength to fight through most of his problems. What he could not fight off was this other "beast" that the drugs unleashed. "I am pretty much scared of everything and trust nothing at this point," was one of the last things he ever wrote. My baby tried. He really tried. He had no idea the thing he thought would make him feel better would ultimately lead him to his death.

We now live with the pain of missing him. *Every. Single. Day.* I wish this pain on no one. It has torn my heart in two. So many people's lives have been affected by Jacob's death. My 20-year-old firstborn son should have lived to get married, achieve his dream of buying a house with land, and have kids. He should have been here with his family for Thanksgiving and Christmas. He should have been here for his youngest brother's first piano recital. He should be making memories with friends and enjoying life experiences. Jacob's decision to use THC wrecked his mind and ended his life at the age of 20. Jacob's death has changed me as a person, as a wife, and as a mother. I long for the earlier times—the time when I was a mother with a full and happy heart; the time I had beautiful, happy boys; and the time when I was a mother of three.

CHAPTER 7:
Never Give Up

TODAY, THINGS ARE GETTING BETTER. A lot better. I want to start there, to offer hope and encourage you not to give up.

My husband and I spent nine days in our son's hospital room. EEG sensors were glued to his head. He couldn't speak. When my son was not tearing apart his room, he stared with vacant eyes. In that hospital room, my husband planned our son's funeral. That was our son's fourth hospitalization.

The first hospitalization was the hardest. His psychosis was severe, and we understood little about psychosis and addiction.

Before everything went wrong, our son was in a doctoral PsyD program and engaged to his high school sweetheart. We were proud of him, excited for them, and delighted for us because they were living nearby. Then COVID shut down everything. He began using marijuana more often, particularly Delta-8. We sensed something was off. But then again, the whole world was off. In August 2020, campus security called us. Our son was wandering around campus and not making sense. When questioned, he'd handed the officer a business card. "Call my dad," he said, acting as if the card gave him license to be there.

We went to campus and pulled into an empty parking lot. Two security officers stood near my son. He had gone to campus looking for a professor, but she wasn't there. Campus was closed because of COVID. He stood by his fiancée's car—door open and motor running. I went to hug him. He backed away, looking distressed, and said, "I don't know who you are." He ranted about the officers, saying, "They put a dead mouse by a dumpster to upset me." He added, "I bought candy to feed to the homeless." He didn't make sense.

After some debate, our son let us drive him to his apartment. We prodded and pleaded, "What are you taking? You're ruining your life. Get help."

He resisted. "I'm smart," he said. "I'm an adult. I can make my own decisions."

His fiancée defended him. "He's stressed," she said. "The doctoral program is hard. He'd be fine if you'd left him alone."

After this episode, things continued to progress. We learned professors and students reported he acted with grandiosity in classes and study groups; he acted like he was the teacher. He was talkative, inappropriately so. The school asked him to withdraw. Someone alerted the police Crisis Intervention Team (CIT). CIT called him and us, suggesting hospitalization. We stalled.

In September 2020, CIT came to his apartment. He agreed to go with them to the hospital. The emergency department (ED) sent him to a psychiatric facility. We couldn't visit due to COVID. Staff provided little information. We called him on the facility's phone. At first, he sounded okay. Then, he trailed off during conversations. Then, he stopped taking our calls.

He began behaving oddly, like wearing his shirt as pants. The staff laughed at him instead of responding to his worsening condition. A concerned night-shift intern called and told us our son had been transferred to a medical hospital because he was suffering from dehydration and "extrapyramidal symptoms." I had no idea what this meant, but I soon learned.

The psychiatric facility had given him multiple types of antipsychotics, which precipitated serotonin syndrome or neuroleptic malignant syndrome (NMS). It's a serious, life-threatening drug reaction. Nothing to be laughed at.

He couldn't lie still. He hadn't slept or had food or water in days. He was hallucinating. He petted imaginary animals and cradled them in his arms. He ripped out his hydration IV again and again. He kept trying to escape, so a "sitter" kept him from leaving. The hospital's only course of treatment was withholding medications in hopes of relieving the NMS.

Despite its negligence, the psychiatric facility repeatedly called the nurses' station, asking them to return my son to the psychiatric facility as soon as he was stable. I stepped out of his room and slid to the floor in tears, overwhelmed, horrified. A nurse came over and whispered, "They killed my brother. Do not send him back!"

My experience with psychiatric facilities was limited to watching *One Flew Over the Cuckoo's Nest*. My son's experience in this facility confirmed the movie and destroyed our faith in the psychiatric system.

Thank God our son lived. He got a job but kept using THC, so he had difficulty concentrating. He believed "undiagnosed ADHD" caused this. A general practitioner apparently accepted our son's self-diagnosis and prescribed different ADHD stimulants, without assessing him. These medications accelerated his psychosis.

In April 2021, his fiancée abruptly left. She texted to me, "When you see him, can you say I love him and he's a good person, but I think we should be apart for each of our mental health." My son was despondent.

In June 2021, our son moved to start a master's program. He wanted a fresh start. He stopped answering my calls and texts, so we drove to check on him. He wasn't attending classes because "the cameras" were watching him. And he said of the cars with Texas license plates, "Those are the ones sending signals to me." He stayed away from televisions, phones, and electronics.

We moved with him to our hometown to be close to our extended family. After a couple of months without medication, alcohol, or THC, he improved. As he improved, our arguments worsened. "I don't want to live with you guys," he said. "I have my own life," he said. But he had no money.

He took a job as assistant manager at a pizzeria and rallied briefly. With the first paycheck, he began vaping Delta-8. "I'm an adult, and this is legal," he said. "If it's legal, it must be safe." The pizzeria demoted him to a driver and eventually fired him.

Life halted. He'd soak in the bathtub for hours with the lights off—no soap or shampoo, though, and the same dirty clothes went back on. His phone lay dead for days. He rarely spoke. He left the house only to get Delta-8.

My husband took our son's car keys. Furious, he called the police and said we stole his car. The police might have acted but saw my husband's name on the car's title.

Our son paced and paced, making triangles between his room, the bathroom, and his car. Attempts to talk with him were met with silent glares or explosions of anger.

"You need help," we said.

"You don't understand!" he snapped. We understood. We witnessed THC's addictive grip on him, engulfing his life and overtaking ours.

Desperate, I visited his therapist. "Can you come to our house?" I pleaded.

"He's an adult," he said. "If he doesn't want help, there's nothing you can do."

"Get help or be evicted," we said. When we told our son to leave, he called the police. They said he could not be kicked out without a 30-day eviction process.

During Christmas week in 2021, he drove away. Voices told him to drive. The voices told him to check into a motel and stay five nights and lie completely still in the bed. They threatened to stop his heart if he didn't comply.

When our son returned home, I was relieved but scared. I didn't see a way out. If we evicted him, I feared he'd kill himself or be lost to the streets. If he stayed, nothing would change. I became numb. I stopped talking to family and friends. I felt embarrassed, humiliated, and defeated. I gained weight. My heart started fluttering and racing. I hoped a heart attack would end my nightmarish existence.

My husband arranged a meeting with a therapist, and I detailed our son's story. He said two things I'll never forget. First, things would have to get worse before they could get better. And second, things might never get better. Then, he looked me in the eye and said, "You need your own therapist." His first remark terrified me; the second angered me. I came to help my son. I bristled when he said *I* needed a therapist.

Seeing a therapist, however, was the most important step of my journey. She gave me hope, clarified my options, and helped me take care of myself— to gain the strength and courage I needed to help my son. I also attended Al-Anon, gardened, and went back to church. I was grateful to God for my wonderful life after both of my boys were born, but I had parted ways with God when I felt my prayers for help went unanswered.

My therapist clarified options for helping my adult son, who refused to help himself. I could petition the Board of Mental Health to have him taken to a psychiatric facility. I could file an eviction petition and hope he'd hit "rock bottom" and get help. Or I could do nothing.

Doing nothing, I discovered, didn't help my son and wreaked havoc on the rest of our family. I filed both petitions. The Board acted immediately. Police took him away in handcuffs, but no one would tell me where he ended up. I was frantic. I found an attorney by searching the state bar's website, and she helped me get temporary guardianship and figure out where he was.

In the hospital, he improved with antipsychotic medication, but miracles don't happen overnight with psychosis. My attorney advised me to insist on a "discharge planning meeting" with his psychiatrist, nurses, psychiatric techs, and social worker. We arranged for him to attend the Salvation Army's mental health respite program and laid out options for what could follow.

My son begged me to let him come home. Seeing his improvement and hopeful we could return to a normal life, we agreed. He met weekly with the psychiatrist who had treated him in the hospital and with a new therapist. He eventually asked to take a community college class.

By summer 2022, though, he had stopped taking risperidone and was overtaking anti-anxiety meds and antidepressants. He asked the psychiatrist for new meds and increased doses. He claimed to have increasing anxiety and other symptoms, and he requested prescription drugs he had researched. He was prescribed an addictive benzodiazepine. Within a week, we found him face down with an empty bottle of prescription benzos nearby.

In the ED, he screamed and yelled at me. The staff asked me to leave because he was disturbing everyone. They had my guardianship papers, but when I called a couple of hours later, they said he'd been discharged. He had no money, no wallet, no phone, and no transportation. I found him on a bench outside a supermarket several blocks from the hospital.

His psychiatrist suggested a long-acting injectable antipsychotic medication, and my son agreed. It was a game changer. With steady doses of medication, he became clearer and clearer. He got a job at Walgreens.

With paychecks, he returned to Delta-8. How could he fear psychosis, know Delta-8 caused it, and still use it? Addiction is a beast.

November 2022 brought the third hospitalization, and Christmas of 2022 brought the fourth. Early in the morning, he knocked on our bedroom door, unable to talk, hardly able to walk, and with fear in his face. We thought he was having a stroke. He collapsed in the emergency department and had severe seizures. He lost control of his bodily functions. Doctors and pharmacists ruled out every possibility but one—substance abuse.

The psychiatrists and neurologists agreed our son needed long-term inpatient treatment. He agreed to go, but no beds were available. By now, we'd changed. We said being at home wasn't helping him. While he waited for a bed to open at a treatment center, his choices were a homeless shelter, a hotel, or the streets. He chose a hotel. I gave an Uber driver an extra 50 dollars to ensure he checked in. He checked in, dropped off his bag, walked to a smoke shop, bought Delta-8, and kept walking.

Temperatures hovered around zero degrees. That night was the coldest of 2022.

My husband, other son, and my sister searched for him. I joined them after filing a missing person report. We searched gas stations, restaurants, bars, convenience stores, and hotels. I said he was wearing a furry hat with ear flaps, like Elmer Fudd. One bartender grabbed a hat from behind the counter and said, "You mean this one?" Our son had used their restroom hours earlier.

His brother called his cell phone, and he answered. When asked where he was, he said, "I see a fire station." My husband drove toward the nearest one. By God's grace, he saw flashing lights and had a feeling it was our son. He was sitting in a police car. A family with children found him in their car after leaving a restaurant. I'm grateful they called the police instead of scaring him off.

The police took him to the hospital. The staff said they'd call when a bed opened. No one called. Our son called from the lobby of a psychiatric facility the next morning. The hospital sent him there in a taxi, but the facility wouldn't admit him. My husband got the admissions nurse on the phone and said, "You have to take him." His medical history, she claimed, indicated his issue was substance abuse, not mental health. My typically mild-mannered husband argued fiercely with her.

Meanwhile, our son simply took an Uber home. I let him in. It was still freezing cold. I called my therapist in tears. She suggested we needed a break until after the holidays. She also said some people don't have rock bottom. I would add people in psychosis lack the ability to ask for help.

The hospital psychiatrist warned us further drug use could kill him, or at the least, it risked permanent psychosis. My son's therapist—with the heartfelt trepidation of a police officer having to tell a parent their child died—delivered his assessment: "He's not ready to quit using Delta-8."

Still determined to get help, I saw an interventionist. Trying to get our business, he predicted that therapy twice a week with him and daily Alcoholics Anonymous (AA) meetings for 90 days would work equally as well as an expensive inpatient treatment facility.

Our son overheard me retelling the advice I was given. A few days later he said he'd do the 90-in-90 (attending a meeting of AA every day for 90 days in a row) and see his current therapist twice a week. This began his path to recovery. He attended AA every single day, sometimes twice a day; I know because I drove him. His seizures prohibited him from driving.

Almost a year later, he finished weaning off his injectable antipsychotic medication. It has been three months since his last injection. It's a scary process because withdrawal symptoms can mimic psychosis, but his brain seems to have adjusted.

Recovery takes a village of competent professionals, supportive friends and relatives, peers who know the journey, parents willing to endure the inevitable setbacks, and the hard work of the person going through the hell of psychosis and the death grip of addiction. It takes faith in God, too.

Christmas of 2023 was wonderful. Our son works as a tutor at a community college and plans to begin a master's program in the fall. He became a certified peer support specialist and accepted a part-time position in a respite program.

When I talk about brain damage done by drugs and psychosis, my son corrects me. He says I should refer to "changes in the brain," not "brain damage." What we both mean is there is no return to baseline. However, the brain can rewire itself. Recovery is possible. I think my kid might make it. Your prayers are appreciated.

CHAPTER 8:

A Rare Success Story

THIS IS A STORY WITH A HAPPY ENDING, but happy endings are not always the case for young adults who become addicted to high-potency THC products. Our family's journey has been full of confusion, fear, and devastation. As parents, we had to do so many hard things; we were not ready to give up on our son. Today, he's on his way to making much better choices.

My son will soon be 20 years old. In spring 2023, his father and I realized he was using marijuana because we smelled the strong odor coming from his room. Of course, he lied when I approached him about it, so I searched his room while he was at school. I found weed, flower buds, small containers of what I later discovered was Delta-8, wax, and vaping cartridges. I destroyed all of it.

Soon afterward, our son experienced a psychotic episode in his high school principal's office. He ran out of the school. Because we have Life360 on our son's phone, we were able to find him and bring him home. My brother-in-law, who is a psychologist, referred us to a local medical facility for an assessment the same day. He had another psychotic episode while there, requiring security to be called. These episodes of psychosis were scary for everyone.

At this assessment, we discovered his THC use had thrown him into psychosis, something we knew absolutely nothing about. We felt like we were on an island, alone. We were confused and terrified. We relied heavily on the expertise of the facility's staff regarding cannabis-induced psychosis (CIP). The psychiatrist suggested he enter an intensive outpatient program (IOP) with teenagers experiencing the same issues. The program included drug testing each week. THC was the only drug for which he ever tested positive. Each week, the amount of THC in his system decreased, but his behavior remained erratic and sometimes volatile. The staff said high-potency marijuana is "killing our youth of today." They explained our son had become addicted to the incredibly high amounts of THC in the Delta-8 cartridges and wax products he had been using, and the effects were usually long-lasting. We were devastated to discover how harmful these drugs were for our son.

His father and I established clear and strict boundaries. We required our son to sign documents allowing us to be included in all medical treatments and assessments, to attend and complete the IOP course, to submit to regular random drug testing, and to remain on lockdown at home until he tested negative. We closely monitored our home security system to ensure he didn't try to leave or allow others to bring him drugs. We were told marijuana typically takes 30 days or more to exit the body. That was a conservative estimate; it took 75 days for the THC to leave our son's body!

Our son graduated from the IOP in four weeks, and afterward, he continued one-on-one therapy. He had been attending a private Catholic high school, so it was up to the principal to decide if he would be allowed to graduate. We pled with the principal, advocating for our son. He knew our son had been a happy-go-lucky, humorous, well-mannered, and charming kid before his psychotic break, and he agreed to let our son complete his final three classes online to graduate from high school. We thanked God for this.

Surprisingly, our son maintained a 3.0 GPA even though we had to nearly fistfight to get him out of bed for school. He often had diarrhea and vomiting, which we now know was hyperemesis caused by his THC use. I have since learned cannabinoid hyperemesis syndrome is common among long-term marijuana users. On his road to recovery, our son worked hard and graduated with an almost 4.0 GPA, and although he could not participate in graduation ceremonies due to the episode at school, we are very proud of him for finishing strong! Perhaps most importantly, he is proud of himself.

In his school's parent newsletter, I noticed an article about a mother from Colorado who had experienced many of the same things we had experienced, and she was coming to speak near our home. That mama was Laura Stack! I cried when I read Laura's story about her son, Johnny, and their family's journey with CIP. Suddenly, I felt we were no longer on an island by ourselves, and I signed our family up to hear her speak. We all looked forward to meeting Laura in person and hearing more!

After hearing Laura speak, our son talked for hours about the information she shared—what he learned and how much of a connection he felt to everyone there dealing with this same problem. He expressed, "Man, this was such an eye-opening experience! I had no idea so many other people have been affected by this too. I don't feel so alone anymore. Thank you so much for making me go to this, Mom." He couldn't stop talking about all the similarities between Johnny Stack's experience and his own. He even said, "Mom, Mrs. Stack may as well have been talking about me tonight with everything she described about Johnny. It's like he and I were the same person in so many ways."

My son's recovery journey has not been straightforward. After several months of sobriety and testing clean, he experienced outbursts and randomly said inappropriate things, which told us he still had a lot of healing to do. Fortunately, he wanted help. He said he was done with marijuana and wanted to heal his brain. I tried my best to believe that my son was really done using it, but my trust had been severed on so many levels. I took away his car, his phone, all cash, and a stack of gift cards he was using to order this junk off the internet. One night, I had to put him into "lockdown" after he became so volatile and belligerent; I was frightened for my life. I called the police for help, but he ran from home before they arrived. I was hoping they could talk to him and maybe scare some sense into him. The choice I was given was to have him arrested. I instead chose to give him another chance, and in this case, I'm glad I did.

I am learning so much from being a part of Laura Stack's Facebook group "Parents of Children with Cannabis-Induced Psychosis." It breaks my heart that so many families are facing the huge challenges brought on by this easily accessible drug.

After much research, I found a therapist near our home who specializes in CIP, and my son began treatment with her in June 2023. I am thrilled to say he has been THC-free for more than nine months now, and we have seen extraordinary changes in his behavior, attitude, appetite, and thought process. His therapist has raved about his progress. She suggested that I could allow my son to begin to earn back my trust by slowly giving him more opportunities to have some independence and some of the freedoms his father and I had taken away while he was using THC. For example, he can now drive himself to his therapy appointments. Of course, he knows I will be watching him on Life360. He travels the 6 miles to therapy and straight back again and does great! It is these small wins that lead to bigger success. As we rebuild trust, I continue to test him randomly every week or 10 days. Overall, he has demonstrated he can remain sober, and he is adamant his THC use was a terrible mistake, and he doesn't want that lifestyle.

This progress led me to suggest something that shocked even me:

I allowed him to stay home alone for a weekend while I traveled out of state to visit my other son and my new grandbaby. I'm so proud to say he did so well! He attended his cousin's wedding and festivities with his dad, who lives seven blocks from us. He cared for our pets and did laundry. I left him with a list of my expectations, and he followed them to a T! Again,

I kept a close eye on him through Life360 and our security system, and he was aware I was monitoring him. This was a huge step for both of us. I was filled with anxiety during that weekend, but I am so super proud of the way he handled himself!

His therapist, his father, and I all suggested he take a year off from higher learning to work and to give his brain and body time to heal further. He has high aspirations for entering a trade school course for aviation mechanics. His brain seems to be nearly 100 percent healed, but it has taken nine long months to get this far. We are stunned at the significant and long-lasting impact his Delta-8 THC vaping, dabbing, and smoking marijuana had on his brain. I'm sharing our family's horrible experiences to help others understand that using today's THC products is dangerous and has changed our lives in ways we never expected or wanted. I know our son has been lucky to be able to recover.

As for me, I am now a State of Indiana Ambassador for Johnny's Ambassadors and am working hard to keep this poison out of the hands of everyone in our community. Thank you to John and Laura Stack for being such wonderful advocates! I pray God continues to bless you in all your endeavors!

CHAPTER 9:

From 420 to 911

MY SON—AT AGE 29—had three episodes of THC psychosis. The hardest part in writing my story is sharing my guilt, shame, and portion of responsibility. My family and I were "responsible" marijuana users and advocates for its legal use for seven years. Even though I quit using marijuana before our son's first psychotic event, I didn't realize THC was the cause at first. Beforehand, we ruled out demonic possession, a bad mushroom trip, and a traumatic breakup as the reason for his psychosis. We thought marijuana was safe until all our 420s (a weed slang term) turned into 911s.

I tried weed in the '80s. My friends and I smoked weed sometimes on weekends at parties, with the only symptoms being heavy eyelids, giggles, and munchies. I wasn't much into it, as I was in a dance company. Weed was around in college. It was there when I toured as a professional dancer, worked for a motion picture company, and later, worked for a law firm. Weed was always somewhere, but it still wasn't my thing. Later, I met my husband, a musician, who liked to smoke weed. His smoking weed didn't bother me for a few years, but later, when we had marital problems, he stopped weed cold turkey. His withdrawals were minor—he was grumpy and irritable for a bit—but then weed-free for over two decades.

Us as a Family

We were a close and engaging family, and we enjoyed raising our son. Spending family time together, being present for his swim meets and soccer games, and traveling to martial arts events was a priority. Running a martial arts school was great for his disciplinary upbringing and kept us close as a family. We cheered for his wins, and cheered louder in his defeats, because win or lose, he was our son.

In adulthood, he became a wonderful teacher, coach, and personal trainer, which kept us—his parents—in shape. He eventually took over our studio, which my husband was building, and I returned to school. He made our school more successful than before, and we were proud of him as a son and grateful to him as an instructor.

Weed Enters the Family

Our son had suffered a serious spleen injury at the age of 17 at a tournament, which took him out of athletics for a year. It was frightening, but he healed quickly and bounced back into athletics faster than most. He also started using weed. When he told us, we didn't freak out as we'd both used weed and moved on from it. We didn't think it was addicting or that anyone had ever died from it. Thus, we were more concerned with alcohol. Whether it was weed or alcohol, we had clear conversations with our son saying that if he was away from home and had too much, he should call us at any hour, and we'd pick him up.

In his 50s, my husband got a "medical" marijuana card for his sciatica. He used it at night, as he was working during the day, so it didn't really bother me. Marijuana was growing in legality, and everyone I knew—from dentists, attorneys, and psychologists to women with hormone issues—were on the healthy weed bandwagon. And eventually, so was I.

In 2012, at age 49, I ruptured my carotid artery. I was in the ICU for a week and at home for months. I had severe migraines and was on pain meds for several years. The opioid crisis was growing as was the healthy marijuana alternative campaign. One was no longer available, and one was gaining acceptance. So, I switched to marijuana.

Weed seemed a lot stronger than I remembered in the '80s. So strong I couldn't indulge until I was showered, the kitchen was clean, and I was in my pajamas, ready for bed. It took some getting used to, but I eventually looked forward to it every night, even if I didn't need it for pain.

Weed became my euphoric escape into bliss and peace. I bought a butter machine to make THC oil, my own capsules, baked goods, and salves for sore muscles and skin problems. Whenever we were in states with legal marijuana, we visited opulent dispensaries for chocolate bars, portable pens, gummies, and nighttime tablets. Our family enjoyed a seven-year 420 relationship. We ate healthy, worked out hard, and enjoyed marijuana at night. But after a few years of using it, I developed depression.

My depression got worse. I started having suicidal ideation and was prescribed antidepressants. My prescriber was a psychiatric nurse and legal marijuana grower. My therapist was a family counselor as well as a substance abuse counselor. She was the first to share that today's weed was more addictive, and some people were having trouble quitting. I used it only at night, so I didn't think I was addicted. And I never considered it was triggering my depression. Still, after the lockdowns, we all wanted to cut weed out for a while and soon realized it wasn't so easy.

When lockdown ended, we wanted to clean up our diet and cut out weed, alcohol, and sugar. Three days into Sober October, our dog died. The boys gave up on sobriety, and I followed less than a week later. We'd try again on New Year's. But chaos began emerging in our close family. Our son had a bad breakup, got intoxicated, drove his car into a ditch, and was lucky to be alive. Worse, he blamed us, as we had seen red flags in his relationship and said something to him. Our good intentions to our beloved son were a huge mistake because he had anxiety and paranoia beforehand, and we didn't realize it—probably because we all had it and didn't realize it at the time. We were all using weed, and it was starting to turn on each of us, and we couldn't see it. Even after three months of quitting weed, sugar, and wine—cold turkey—and witnessing my son's first psychotic event, I didn't get the connection.

One day, he came out of his room a total stranger. It was like he had a dark entity inside of him. In fact, he said he did. He said God was talking to him, had given him knowledge and the ability to see evil in others. He spoke in a dark, emotionless voice, and his eyes were dilated. He had a twitch of extremely fast and disturbing high-pitched laughter—like a character in a horror movie—that came at unusual moments. It was clear he was having a mental health emergency, and it was beyond disturbing. His movements were slow, and his head was tilted down.

Besides the knowledge from God, he said a blue goddess was inside him as well. I learned later other THC-psychosis sufferers had similar experiences. He told us in a rage we needed to be cleansed of evil. Although in shock, we learned quickly to be as calm with him as possible, in order not to provoke him. And while my husband stayed with him, I went upstairs and called 911, because whoever came out of that room wasn't our son.

At the suggestion of the dispatcher, we sedated him with a sedative, and eventually he calmed down. He was incoherent and nonresponsive, but he was no longer shouting and enraged. I asked the police—who'd been parked in the driveway—to leave. That night, we all slept on the huge recliner sofa—including the dog—surrounding our son like a blanket, and we prayed for a miracle. The following morning, I took him to the hospital.

"Does Your Son Use Marijuana?"

He woke up "our son" again—lucid, responsive, but not remembering much of what had happened. He said the night before was like a dream. When I drove to the hospital, I stayed outside—due to COVID rules—which was horrible after what had happened. When the doctor called me, he asked, "Does your son smoke marijuana?" He said young men were showing up in emergency departments around the U.S. with similar symptoms, and they all had THC in their systems. I told him he'd been depressed after a bad breakup and a week ago tried mushrooms to feel better, and he did. He was happier for an entire week. The doctor said, "Marijuana could be triggering psychosis, and it's happening more than people realize. If he used marijuana even hours before coming out of his room with psychosis, that could be the cause." He'd used mushrooms over a week ago but had psychosis yesterday right after using weed.

Much later, I learned through education that psychosis isn't an illness; it's a symptom of something else. Psychosis is often a symptom of serious mental illness, such as bipolar disorder or schizophrenia. Sometimes, using THC can trigger psychosis in people who have not previously shown signs of serious mental illness. Psychosis triggered from using THC does not always go away even if the THC usage stops.

We didn't understand any of this at the time and had to learn the hard way. When we got home from the hospital, my husband never touched weed again. Our son stopped using weed as well, but unfortunately for only a short time. With so many people using marijuana and mistakenly believing it is safe, he had a lot of cognitive dissonance.

I researched everything about marijuana psychosis after that. I was finishing a degree at OSU online, enrolled in a course called Psychology of Addiction, and with my professor's help, did my final research project on the neurotoxicity of high-potency THC. I read reports about hospitals experiencing increases in young adults with THC psychosis, and I read hundreds of family horror stories. The symptoms were like our son's, and the personality changes were spot on. My son's brain couldn't handle weed anymore. And every time he used it after his first psychosis, he spiraled downward into delusion, paranoia, and anger. It was hard to get him to stop as he didn't believe weed was the culprit, or maybe he just couldn't quit. And I was hitting a wall trying to get him help as there was no mental health help available for a month due to post-COVID challenges. Everyone needed help, and we were put on waiting lists.

One night, he was blasting music past midnight and talking to himself—vacillating between anger and laughter. I woke in the morning to check on him. I found him sitting outside, listless in a chair, with drawings, numbers, and words—from head to toe—all over his body from an ink marker. I held back tears as I wiped the writing off his arms and head with a warm towel. His suffering was breaking me. He needed help so badly. I called the crisis center, but they didn't get back to me. So, I called my therapist for help. She told me she'd retired due to the death of her daughter. After I told her what had happened, she told me her daughter passed away after eating THC edibles. She became psychotic and died by suicide a few hours later. I was horrified. Was this going to happen to my son? I didn't stop calling the crisis center until a social worker finally came out. When the social worker showed up, our son was dissociative, and the social worker promised to get him help as soon as she could. It never came, even after more phone calls. Two weeks later, we were crying in our cars, searching for our son everywhere after he left for a run and didn't return.

I went into his room and found his phone and watch. After almost two hours, I started looking for him. I drove all his running routes, couldn't find him, called my husband, and we split up and searched in different areas. I posted on a local alert page, and somebody spotted him running down the highway. He ran 15 miles along the highway—in 80-plus degrees of island heat—into town. I found him at our studio, severely agitated, and he was worse when we got home. He was verbally abusive, delusional, and yelling at my husband. He was making irrational demands and threats. We told him that we'd either drive him to the hospital or call the police. But he was out of control.

When the police came, he made a run for the fence line, but an amazing and gentle policewoman caught up with him and got him to listen to her. She got him to walk with her back up to the cars. I told her a brief history: no violence, no crime—just weed—and he'd never been like this before his psychosis. She told me they were dealing with this a lot, and they needed more help for mental health emergencies like this. Young people had psychosis, families were scared, and weed was often the only substance involved. With her help, our son went voluntarily to the hospital.

The hospital psychiatrist diagnosed him with bipolar disorder and placed him on antipsychotics. (This was a year before research showed high THC could cause bipolar disorder.) He also told my son he needed to stop using weed and why, and the advice seemed to work. When we got home, he grabbed everything downstairs that was weed-related and gave it to us. The antipsychotics—although important at first—were harsh, filled with horrendous side effects, and halted his life completely. We got the psychiatrist to switch the meds, but he still felt horrible. I helped him taper off them gradually by adding other brain supplements I'd researched myself.

Using my research background, I explored how to help my son. I gave him a clean diet, and alternative supplements nurtured his brain, mood, and especially his neurotransmitters. After a month, he started improving, and we were feeling positive. I connected with a neuroscientist in Europe who provided me with more data on other potential brain supplements as well. He used them, with marked improvement. What I couldn't do was get him to realize the harm THC was doing to his brain.

I sent him links and articles—without nagging or pleading—in hopes he'd change his perspective. I lost sleep and went without food for long periods due to constantly researching and reading past midnight. I was obsessed and driven to get my son healed. Even though I'd been getting healthier, my depression was getting worse due to weight loss and lack of sleep. My own brain was about to crash, and I was too obsessed with research and worry to realize it. Ignoring my therapist's warning to keep tabs on my health, I had a complete mental breakdown and spent several nights in the hospital.

I woke up one morning with immeasurable guilt over what had happened to my son. I was physically numb. I was experiencing a dark night of the soul in which self-hatred, guilt, and shame overcame me, and I was swallowed by darkness. I was a horrible mother whose son was suffering due to my ignorance, and in my twisted mind, my physical presence was the culprit. Almost four months after quitting high-potency THC products, I had the worst suicidal ideation imaginable, and it caused even more chaos. It was also proof—to outsiders—that weed was not to blame; I was.

I drove to the emergency department dehydrated, sleep deprived, and 20-plus pounds underweight. The psychiatrist who dealt with my son was now dealing with his sleep-deprived train wreck mother, who now—besides being guilt-driven—had the shame of not being able to hold it together. I hit bottom. But something occurred that took the edge off my ego death. Other doctors who knew our family and heard I was admitted started popping into my room during waking hours and sharing their stories of struggle. One had a son and another a nephew, and they both developed schizophrenia from marijuana. Another doctor shared their breakdown, and some stories were too personal to ever share, but their vulnerability in sharing took the edge off my personal guilt and shame. Afterward, I made time for my own healing, started meditating, going to support groups, and learned to give whatever I couldn't change up to God. I still had a lot of chaos before me, but I was now out of my own way.

Many believed THC wasn't the bad guy, we were—and so we lost friends. While we had become adamant against weed, our son didn't believe weed caused his psychosis and blamed us for much of what had happened. He needed allies, and some of the friends we had lost became his confidants. He told them it was bipolar disorder, not weed, and that we were overreacting.

All we could do was be accountable, make amends, and not defend ourselves too much. We were accomplices, after all. Thus, defending ourselves seemed futile. His mental health was more important, so we learned not to take anything personally. Having dealt with my own substance abuse, I knew the power of denial, as well as agitation against anyone who objects to that substance. Telling somebody not to do something they want to do is futile. I accepted that I couldn't change my son and gave the hard days up to God. My husband and I became more involved at our school and started working out and meditating regularly. Our son's mood improved, he became more physically active as well, and we all started getting along better. Still, he slipped one more time.

His last psychosis event happened the night after the funeral of a childhood friend. A family friend lost his daughter to an accidental overdose. While our son was out on the boat with the father, spreading his daughter's ashes, my husband and I stood on the shore, with me crying. Would this one day happen to us? Late in the evening, after spending time with friends, our son came home in psychosis and rage. It was the worst event to date. We gave him a sedative and stayed with him until he went to sleep. In the morning, when he was lucid and responsive, we implemented our rules and boundaries. After the funeral, and later the psychosis, we realized tough boundaries were all we had left. We warned him of random drug tests, banning him from teaching, and more. Establishing these boundaries ended up being the best strategy of all.

He tapered down to CBD (with less than 0.003 percent THC), which kept him from depression, cravings, and withdrawals. He started doing jiujitsu again, where he was surrounded by positive role models, like police and firefighters. He started working out hard again and later reconnected with a friend from college, a weed-free woman who was smart and headstrong and had a good career. I never saw so much change in him. I never thought I'd see my son happy and motivated again. He learned how to self-regulate and monitor his mental health and started researching on his own what supplements to take and what to avoid for cognitive balance.

Last year, he won gold at a jiujitsu event—an incredible victory for a warrior back up on his feet again. This year, three of his taekwondo athletes medaled at the U.S. Open. He now lives with his girlfriend, who recently became his fiancée, and visits us every week. I'm proud of how hard he's worked to heal his life, and I'm so grateful our family was able to rebuild after incredible mental and emotional hardship.

Looking Back

It's been two years since I quit THC, which I used for nearly seven years. It took a year to recover and for depression to disappear. While using high-potency THC, my personality, behavior, and mental health were severely impinged upon. Neither I nor my husband realized how much weed had affected our behavior until long after we were clean. It's like we woke up from a dream, losing an entire decade. What it did to our son—in his late 20s—was so much worse.

We each tried many times to quit but couldn't. We had to suffer total breakdowns before we could experience any breakthroughs. Most people still don't think high-potency weed is toxic to the brain, and many still don't believe it's responsible for what our family endured. Some people I've shared our story with eventually quit and have had life-changing experiences, while others have begun to realize quitting weed is not so easy.

Weed is everywhere. I smell it on the roadways every time I run, and it affects me like a war veteran. Still, I'm not anti-cannabis—CBD helped my son detox off the hard stuff—but I wish more people knew about the deception of high-potency THC products. It is unfortunate many will have to learn the hard way.

"There are two ways to be fooled. One is to believe what isn't true; the other is to refuse to believe what is true." —Søren Kierkegaard

CHAPTER 10

THC Turned My Son Into Someone I Did Not Know

I AM THE DIVORCED MOTHER of a 22-year-old son. I live in Colorado where marijuana was legalized for recreational use in 2012.

Even before THC took over our lives, life was challenging as a divorced mother. I was my son's sole physical and emotional support. His father was in and out of our son's life, providing minimal financial assistance. Those days were easy compared to what was to transpire.

My son was diagnosed with ADHD when he was 6. He was doing quite well with therapy and medication. He attended a private school in Denver that specialized in kids with learning challenges. Growing up, my son was always empathetic. He had a big heart for the people around him and would help wherever and whenever. He was very paternal and loved working with younger children. His creative mind was always in overdrive. He was artistic and was always drawing. He thought outside of the box and was an excellent problem solver, often coming up with novel ideas and solutions. He was independent from an early age. He always wanted to find his own way around and do things himself, which was both a blessing and a curse because he never accepted suggestions or directions.

At 16, my son began infrequently using high-potency marijuana. At 17, he discontinued his ADHD medication and started using THC much more frequently. He believed all the hype claiming that marijuana was the cure-all for everything. It was not long before he used marijuana daily and then progressed to multiple times a day. I found dabs in his room, as well as apples, flowers, spoons, tinfoil, pipes, etc. Dabbing, which involves heating highly concentrated wax and inhaling the vapors, was his preferred modality.

I watched his behavior morph into something unrecognizable, and I slowly caught on to his usage. I did some research and learned what THC could do to the developing brain. He was highly combative, violent, unmotivated, and extremely paranoid. He was convinced Nazis were out to get him. His therapist counseled him on these effects, but because he had already developed a substance abuse disorder with marijuana, no amount of discussion or reason had any influence on him.

His GPA went from a 2.85 to a 1.5. He graduated from high school only because an administrator dragged him across the finish line by having him focus on passing one class. My son had been accepted to college at Fort Lewis in Durango, Colorado. This was the school he'd wanted to attend since he was 12, but now he had absolutely no motivation to go. He caused $4,000 worth of damage to my house, including broken windows and holes in the walls. There were burn marks on the carpeting in his room from dabbing and using oils, as well as burn holes in the rug in the family room.

At times, his violence was directed at me. While he never hit me, he pushed me. He got in my face and yelled and cursed at me. He even clutched a kitchen knife during an argument, though I don't know what he intended to do with it. I was fearful for my physical safety. I never knew what to expect when I came home. I was always walking on eggshells. My life was unpredictable and chaotic. I was no longer living in "my" house. My son and his addiction had taken over.

I set many consequences for my son. I followed through on every one of them. He was forbidden to use marijuana in my house. I took his phone and tablet. No socializing with friends. I removed his bedroom door, telling him he couldn't have privacy if he couldn't be trusted. He drove his car twice while high on THC, so I sold it. He did not care and used marijuana anytime he wanted.

On several occasions, I called the police. I begged them to take my son to juvenile detention, but they never would. They would give him a stern talk, but there were never legal consequences. He threatened to kill himself and was taken on the first of many 72-hour revolving-door holds. My son learned he could continue to do whatever he wanted in my home, and no one could stop him.

He stole from me. He would take cash from my wallet. He learned how to forge a check online. Since I had sold his car, he felt he had the right to steal my car. It got to a point where I was sleeping with my wallet and my car keys. I should have filed charges against him for theft. I was simply so stunned by his behavior that I did not think of filing charges at that time. Perhaps had I filed charges, I could have prevented what happened next.

Six months before his 18th birthday, I gave him an ultimatum: "If you want to continue to live in my house, you will abide by my rules, or you will be evicted." I would have to go through the eviction process since my address was on his driver's license.

The rules I put in place were:

1. Respect my property and me.
2. Be a full- or part-time student.
3. If you are not going to school, work full-time and pay rent.
4. You must remain sober, and there will be no drugs on my property.
5. You will go to 12-step meetings three times a week.

I prepared and printed a document of my rules with all the information. When I presented it to my son, he scoffed at me and tossed it aside.

In October 2019, two months after he turned 18, I evicted my son from my home. It was the single worst day of my life. I, again, presented the rules document to him at a public restaurant, as I knew things would get ugly. He said he would comply with some of the rules but refused to go to 12-step meetings or quit using THC. I left him at the restaurant and drove home. Within 10 minutes, he was pounding on the door. I called the police. This time, I had all the proper paperwork in hand. My son tried to show the police his driver's license to convince them he lived there. The police told him he no longer lived in my home. He must pack a bag, and they would take him where he wanted to go, but he must leave now. I kept myself from crying until they were outside the door, and even then, I cried very little. To survive this process, I learned to shove my feelings down and build a thick wall. It served me well during this journey.

Thus began his homeless days, and he was homeless in Denver for a few weeks. He was enjoying it, as his Instagram account showed. Eventually, I got him into a facility that helps young adults in crisis get their feet back on the ground. What he truly needed was months in a dual diagnosis residential treatment center to address both addiction and mental health issues. However, this crisis facility was a safe place where he had access to help. Unfortunately, he continued to use marijuana. He smoked marijuana in his apartment and posted it on Instagram. This was a direct violation of the program. He was so psychotic and paranoid that he would sit in the lobby and accuse other residents of being Nazis. He made two more suicide threats and was taken to a behavioral health facility both times. The second time, he was taken to a mental health facility. He was hospitalized for five days, but because he was an adult, I wasn't notified. After five days, he was released with medication and told to follow up with mental health care. Of course, this was ineffective. A day after he was released, my son told me he was sexually assaulted in this hospital and people were crawling through the air ducts, searching for him. He also claimed the doctors injected him with a green dye that was a virus, and now he was dying. I know this was all psychosis and paranoia caused by THC. This was the first of three incidents where he claimed sexual assault, but none had occurred. Through his journey, I can't even recollect how many attempts he made on his life and how many revolving-door 72-hour holds occurred.

In April 2020, when the world was shut down due to COVID, my son could no longer tolerate the fear of Nazis being after him. He flew to Los Angeles on a cheap plane ticket. He was homeless on the streets of LA or on the beach. One time, he even slept in a dumpster to be safe. He trekked around LA County by bus, getting THC and other substances however he could. He did not have a phone. He would call whenever the kindness of a stranger would allow. Days, weeks, or sometimes months would go by, and I would not hear from him. I was working with LA County officials and shelters to find him. My son was also in and out of jail several times. Due to the COVID shutdown, he wasn't kept in jail. When I learned he was arrested, I would call the police department to see if they could find him. I asked an LAPD officer if I needed to start calling the morgue periodically. The officer told me since my son had been arrested a few times, and they had his photo, "Your son will never be a John Doe." As sick as this sounds, it was comforting.

During Easter week of 2020, I received a phone call from an agent at the federal building on Wilshire Boulevard. My son had thrown a rock through a $10,000 window of the federal building because he did not like Donald Trump. The agent said the building housed 700 to 800 federal agents. The agent told me he knew something was wrong with my son right away, but his hands were tied as to what he could do. He also said my son was only wearing socks, no shoes. He kindly found shoes for my son, but since my son would not consent to go to a hospital, all the agent could do was offer to drive him to a shelter. An agent dropped my son off at a shelter, but my son never walked in. After five months of homelessness, my son showed up on my brother's doorstep. My brother and his family live in LA, but since my son's brain was impaired, he had never thought of going there.

I flew out to California and brought him back home in September 2021.

I hoped this journey would be the beginning of a happy ending, but it was not. My son still refused treatment. The best I could do was to negotiate sober living as a condition. Sadly, he didn't maintain sobriety. He had no intention of doing so, and he was kicked out three times.

In April 2022, my son flew back to LA, beginning round two of homelessness.

In December 2023, he shared with me that he would sing "Boulevard of Broken Dreams" by Green Day to himself as he wandered from Venice to Downtown LA parks. This song is about being utterly alone. This is how my son felt through his addiction. I listen to that song now with deep emotion, picturing my son wandering, homeless and hopeless. I won't put the lyrics here due to copyright, but please look up the song on Google.

At some point, he was hospitalized again. He told the emergency department nurse he had been raped. A physical examination showed no evidence of rape. This was the second psychotic sexual incident. The hospital transferred my son to its sister behavioral health facility. A nurse told me he expected my son to be there for at least a month. I was relieved. I thought he would finally get the help he needed. But after five days, the doctor gave him meds and sent him out the door! My son said he wouldn't hurt himself or others; therefore, they would not keep him. Understand our mental health care system is broken. There are very few beds available, and they need to be filled with patients with cash or very good insurance. However, my son had Medi-Cal. So, from there, he ended up in what I think was a halfway house for help. However, he called to tell me he must leave immediately because they wanted to make porn videos with him (third psychotic sexual incident). He did not even stay one night. Clearly, he was not ready to leave the behavioral health facility because he was still psychotic.

After several more months of homelessness again, he was jailed in Orange County. It took eight months in jail before I could tell my son's head was starting to clear. He was released on probation to a halfway house. Jail was what finally got him clean.

Fast-forward to today. As I write this, it is February 2024. My son celebrated two years of sobriety in November 2023. In June 2023, he graduated from the halfway house to a sober living house, and he will be off probation in April 2024. He attends 12-step meetings regularly. He has finished his first semester of school with good grades. He is studying to be an addiction counselor. He also works part-time and pays for his phone, rent, food, and incidentals. I look forward to visiting him, and we always have a great time together. It has taken two years for me to get my son back! He is now the person he was before he started using THC at 16! It has been six years now, and his future looks bright. It is never lost on me how lucky we are. By all logical reasoning, my son should not be alive. God only knows why he is here.

I want parents to know they need knowledge, boundaries, and hope. THC is potent and should never be referred to as "weed." "Weed" implies it's safe, and it is not safe. The marijuana industry has hidden up to 90 percent of THC in its products, and its goal is to get kids hooked. If parents set a boundary, they must follow through. Enabling or going back on their word is not an option. Addiction is the only disease that destroys not only the hosts but also everyone around them. Parents need to take back their lives and protect everyone, especially their other children in the home. Do not fear jail. Besides knowing the whereabouts of the addicted person, jail may be precisely what their child needs to get clean. Hope will come in many ways, from the kindness of strangers and caregivers to a support group with a 12-step program like Al-Anon. Finally, pray a lot.

CHAPTER 11:

Hindsight is 20/20

MY SON, "C," was an adorable child. Born with very poor eyesight, he looked just like the little boy with spiky hair and big bottle glasses from the *Jerry Maguire* movie. And he had a similarly deep voice and big personality, just like the lovable little actor.

I start my story with C's troublesome eyesight because, even as a young child, it was a barrier to entry into the sports world. C struggled with hand-eye coordination. As a result, he did not enjoy any of the sports his dad and I signed him up to play. He hated baseball. He sat down on the soccer field, picking at the grass. He swam and participated in Junior Lifeguards, but only because we forced him, since we live at the beach and being able to swim is a safety issue in our community.

What C truly loved and excelled at was playing video games. We continued to encourage him to be active, teaching him to surf, taking him camping, skiing, and hiking. But from 3 years old on, C's greatest pleasure came from his screen time.

C had lots of friends. He attended private school and achieved good grades. He was well liked by his peers. He was happy, generally, but as he reached his teen years, he became more reserved and less talkative. He often retreated to his room and the virtual world of video games.

And then came COVID. In eighth grade, C joined millions of kids across this country in the isolation of virtual online learning. Both his dad and I worked full-time, which left C and his sister on their own, trying to survive with little interaction with friends and virtually no in-person social life.

Eighth grade is also when C reported trying marijuana for the first time. I don't know when or where this occurred, but I have learned since that C really, really liked it. By then, he started to pick up skateboarding, and unfortunately, as we learned, smoking marijuana is a prevalent part of skateboard culture. At first, he reported that he smoked infrequently. But by the end of sophomore year, he was smoking regularly with his friends at the skate park on the weekends. Although by then I knew he had smoked a few times, I was naïvely unaware it had become a regular habit for him.

Flash-forward to the summer prior to C's junior year of high school. When C was home, he was isolating himself in his room more and more frequently. One weekend while I was out of town and he was staying at his dad's house, he purchased mushrooms on Instagram, and C had a very scary episode in which he was acting out of control and needed to be restrained. It was then his dad and I learned he was also purchasing marijuana regularly from an online "plug," also known as an "untraceable drug dealer," who he communicated with through Instagram and Snapchat.

As a result of the mushroom incident, we spoke to C repeatedly about the dangers of taking drugs. We hired an antidrug activist and invited him to speak to other parents at his dad's community club. Part of C's "rehabilitation" was we made him get up and speak to all the parents about the mushroom incident and the dangers of purchasing drugs online. We believed the hallucinogenic episode was as frightening for C as it was for us and hoped talking about the ordeal would deter his future drug use and purchasing behavior. We were so naive—C only gave the speech because we made him, and he continued to purchase and smoke marijuana on a regular basis.

Throughout this time, I also was unaware of "dabbing" or of vaping THC. I assumed if C was smoking, it was green bud that would smell, and he would smell like pot after smoking. And of course, because he was vaping, I never smelled it on him.

During the first semester of junior year, C's grades started to slip. He was with his friends more often, was less talkative, and was frequently self-isolated. We always had a pretty good relationship, but then one day, out of the blue, we got into an explosive fight. As I tried to give him pointers related to a job interview, he yelled he hated me and stormed out of the house.

I was flabbergasted. I had never had this type of interaction with any of my children. Later, when we were in a calmer place, he told me he had questions about why his dad and I had divorced, and I immediately scheduled a counseling session for us to speak together with a therapist. I presumed he was growing up and experiencing normal teenage angst over things he hadn't processed properly and simply didn't understand.

The following Sunday morning was our first therapy session. I was supposed to pick him up at his friend's house, where he had spent the night. On my way to him, he texted and called me trying to get out of the session. In the end, he allowed me to pick him up, but he was acting strangely and talking in a nonsensical manner. In retrospect, I can't believe it took me so long to clue in, but I didn't realize he was high. Neither did the therapist.

Later that evening, I tried to help C with a project for his health class, but he was uncooperative. The next morning, as he was brushing his teeth, he calmly explained it was my fault he didn't finish the project. "How is that?" I asked him.

"You didn't stop them from watching me." *Huh?*

"I didn't stop who from watching you?" I asked, genuinely confused.

"The FBI."

I honestly thought my son was pulling my leg. He left for school, and I called his school counselor. I told him my son was acting strangely, his grades were slipping, and I was hoping they could help me with some sort of intervention. He told me he would consult with his team and call me back.

Two hours later, I saw a call coming in from the school and expected it to be the counselor returning my call. Instead, it was the vice principal, informing me C had come to his office, claiming the FBI was following him. C had explained the vice principal was the only person he could trust.

The vice principal found drug paraphernalia in C's backpack. By the time I arrived at school, C was telling the team that had convened he was stuck in a *Rick and Morty* cartoon, life was a simulation, and only he could save the universe from doom.

Two hours later, the emergency department doctors did not hesitate to diagnose my son with THC-induced psychosis, a diagnosis I had not known even existed. I learned my son had vaped high-potency THC that morning and several times in the days preceding the hospitalization. I was in a state of disbelief and stupor. How had this happened under my nose, and how had I failed to see any of it?

C was transferred that evening to a psychiatric facility, where he remained for six days. During that time, his dad and I hit the ground running. We researched the different types of treatment programs available. We decided to send C straight from the hospital to a 90-day wilderness program in Utah.

This was the beginning of a five-month nightmare. C despised the wilderness program, and he complained he was freezing and threatened to kill himself daily. After less than three weeks, the counselors agreed the wilderness program was not the right fit for him, so we had him transferred to an intensive inpatient clinical program, which was also in Utah.

Two days in, to my dismay, I learned his primary counselor at the new treatment program had never heard of THC-induced psychosis. Despite my deep dive into medical research on treating this relatively new diagnosis, I could not figure out whether the antipsychotic and anti-anxiety medications prescribed were even appropriate. C was falling into utter despondency, begging us to take him home.

Fighting ensued between C's dad and me after 18 years of a cohesive co-parenting relationship. C's dad wanted to bring him home. I was adamant he was not better. Ultimately, his dad picked him up less than three weeks after he arrived at the second program.

Within a week, C vaped again. I suffered a panic attack. I was an inconsolable mess.

We struggled to determine the next steps. We tried to force C to enroll in a continuation school program he was dead set against attending. A couple of days before he was scheduled to start at the new school, C swallowed a bottle of Benadryl tablets. Fortunately, we got him to the hospital in time, and he hadn't taken enough to cause permanent damage. He spent three days in the emergency department, as we scrambled for the third time to find an appropriate treatment facility.

C spent the next three months in a local dual diagnosis inpatient facility where we were able to see him weekly and attend in-person family counseling. Those weeks were grueling, as C didn't seem to be making much progress in understanding THC is dangerous, addicting, and a significant root cause for his depression and manic behavior. His depression hung on him for weeks as he continued to beg us to take him home.

It took three months for C to finally wake up and start acting like the teenager we knew before he became addicted to THC. He graduated from the 90-day program, and we brought him home with strict rules and oversight. It has been almost a year, and C is now drug-free and on track to finish high school.

We work on improving our relationship every day. A couple of weeks ago, we scheduled surgery. C is getting implantable contact lenses that will enable him to have almost 20/20 vision for the first time in his life! As we walked out of the doctor's office, C had tears in his eyes and gave me the first real hug I have felt from him in ages.

"Thanks, Mom. I love you," he said.

"I love you too, bud," I responded.

I don't think he can comprehend how much I love him. Nor can he comprehend the magnitude of the loss we almost suffered when we nearly lost him. All of this happened because of THC—a terribly misunderstood and deadly drug.

CHAPTER 12:

Just a Shell

WHEN MY SON WAS 17, I realized he was slowly being erased and all that remained was a shell of a person.

A year and a half earlier, he was hardworking, creative, self-driven, and mature for his age, with so many opportunities ahead. We did our best to provide a healthy environment. As a mom, I was present, accessible, and took great pride in the most important job I ever held. And it came as a shock to see drastic changes in my son—a young man with no ambition, no drive, no rationale, no personality, and no concerns. His grades declined from A's and B's to barely passing.

When he was 16, we knew he was adjusting to coming out of the COVID lockdown, like the rest of the world. We had no idea what was about to follow. He was beginning the natural struggle of becoming independent from us, his parents. We trusted him. Out of our six children, he seemed the most rational and responsible, so we gave him a little more freedom. That all changed shortly before his 17th birthday. We caught him smoking marijuana. I expressed my concern about using drugs and made it clear his dad and I would not allow it. He tried to assure us, saying, "Do you think I'm dumb? I'm not going to do anything addictive!" Knowing the potential reality of the situation, we tested him with a multidrug home urine test, which showed marijuana use. Although I had never used marijuana myself, I told my son I understood well the risks of dependency because as a teen I witnessed my sibling become addicted to marijuana. We shared examples of how marijuana could ruin a person's life. At this point, we really thought he would make better choices and hoped he would return to the rational-minded kid we knew him to be. However, we had no real awareness of the dangers of today's high-potency marijuana. We didn't even know what THC was at the time.

That following spring, we faced more signs that things were not right with my son. We enrolled him in an intensive food allergy program across the country with hopes of putting his anaphylactic food allergy into remission for good. During the visits, his heart rate, blood pressure, and lung function were closely monitored, and each time, the results were inconsistent and abnormal. While the doctors were not overly concerned, it was alarming to me.

During our extensive travels to treatment that summer, I spent more time near my son, where I took notice of unusual behaviors. He was excessively tired, easily annoyed, no longer practiced self-care, and spent a lot of time in bathrooms. During our overnight hotel stays, I noticed very strong fruity smells, night terrors, unsteady shaking hands, stomach issues, decreased appetite, lack of self-control with junk food and drinks, weight loss, and headaches. I dismissed it all to his allergy issues, jet lag, and being a typical 17-year-old.

As I continued to observe what were really the symptoms of drug use, I asked my son to take a drug test, which only led to arguments. My son accused me of not trusting him. After we found his nicotine vape in our bathroom, we insisted on drug testing him again, which he refused. One morning, my husband woke very early for work and noticed a light on in our son's car in the driveway. Our son had passed out in his car surrounded by marijuana, alcohol, and who knows what else.

After all this, I began to feel I was living life in a bad dream I desperately wanted to awake from. I knew in my gut my son was using illicit substances. It all made sense—why I made sure we had Narcan in the house and why I searched through his belongings. It was hard to acknowledge our son had a serious drug problem, and by the time we realized what he was using, it was too late for early intervention.

We found evidence of alcohol, 'shrooms, kratom, and many forms of marijuana, including dabs containing 90 percent-plus THC. We found a journal where our son wrote notes on how to get the "most effective" high by using combinations of different substances. He obtained the THC by direct mail, and because it had no smell, he could easily hide it. Not wanting to give up, we implemented weekly random drug testing, which made no difference in his use. We required him to report to a trusted adult of his choice for additional accountability. This also did not make a difference in his use. We installed cameras in our home for more vigilance. After each positive drug test, we took away privileges one by one, including driving and Wi-Fi access. We pulled him from the allergy program and made him quit his job at a restaurant with a bar and a bad atmosphere. Our life became one of confiscating car keys at night, figuring out potential liability and legal rights as parents of a minor, and educating ourselves on the substances our son was using.

Three months later and three weeks shy of turning 18, our son had no money and was restricted to driving to work and school because of a ticket for excessive speeding. We told him if he continued to use drugs, he would have to leave our home. He had no plan for where to go if he left. None of the consequences mattered to him. My husband warned him, if he continued this path, he would lose everything—his machinist job, his vehicle, his friends.

His 18th birthday came and went, and he was still not sober. Knowing our rules, he moved out two weeks later, taking his belongings, clothes, and his car, which he had purchased himself. I feel guilty saying this, but our home had a sense of peace once he moved out. I had mixed feelings of horrible sadness, but also relief. Within a month after moving out, he was working at the bar again. His car broke down, and he did not repair it, despite the fact he is a gifted mechanic. His mind was not clear enough at this point to diagnose and solve the problem. He also stopped attending school regularly and quit his job as a machinist. He broke off relationships with friends and made new "friends" who shared his lifestyle. He barely managed to graduate from high school five months later. He sent me a paranoid text saying, "I know what you did." I had no idea what he was referring to, and it disturbed me to my core. His substance use was affecting him even more deeply. His old friends reported his use was the heaviest it had ever been.

Another excruciating eight months passed without seeing or speaking to my son. I reached out every two to three days but received no response. Then, there was a glimmer of hope. He called to ask for a document he needed to apply for a job in a warehouse. He avoided seeing me by picking it up after his late shift. He didn't have to call; he could have texted or asked his brother to bring it to him. I like to think he wanted to hear my voice. Hearing his voice was a small gift I now hang on to. He was polite. I was only positive, telling him, "I hope it works out for you" and "I'm so glad to hear that. It's so good to hear your voice."

Unfortunately, things went right back to not hearing from him. I still messaged him every couple of days. He got the job he applied for, but he quit two months later. His creative mind wasn't happy with the mundane tasks of the job. Although his dark struggles continue, I hear from others he's trying to get a stable job as a machinist again. He seems excited to move forward and has another vehicle for transportation. I pray he's on a better path.

It's still a bad dream. I hurt every day. So bad. I feel like I'm drowning. Everyone who knows my son is shocked by his choices. Perhaps my son would still have chosen high-risk behaviors, but if THC was regulated with some real legislation and potency caps, maybe his life wouldn't be in such ruin. How do I get through it? I talk with other families who have loved ones who are also suffering from THC use. I try to do "normal" things, focus on my other kids, and appreciate the many good things I still have. Mostly, how I get through each day is by believing in and worshipping The Living God. I rely on Him heavily through these dark times. I hope one day all this pain and heartache will be gone.

I thank God for people who are tirelessly fighting this fight. The other night my husband prayed to God, saying, "Please, make it hard for my son to get drugs. Put obstacles in his path." If you're reading this story, you can be that obstacle. Educate yourself and help spread the truth that marijuana, especially high-potency THC, is an unregulated dream-killer. It is killing our kids.

CHAPTER 13:
A Hellacious Journey

IN JULY 2002, our firstborn child was a healthy 9-pound baby boy. He learned to walk on his first birthday. He learned to read by age 5. By age 10, he was an athlete who played baseball, football, and hockey. He also skied and snowboarded in the Rocky Mountains. By high school, he was 6 feet tall. He was attending a prestigious private high school. He made the high school football and baseball teams.

In November 2016, he was invited to a sleepover with a few of the team members. When I arrived to pick him up, I remember it took 30 minutes for the host mom to rouse the boys. I was growing frustrated but tried to be polite. They were in the basement, so I didn't see the sleeping arrangements. The home was a beautiful one, in Arvada, an upper-class suburban neighborhood. My assumption was he was safe—especially because he was busy with other athletes—"good" kids. Unfortunately, the boys had found some marijuana, property of an older sibling.

I didn't know it at the time, but that was the beginning of my then 14-year-old son's five-year journey through marijuana addiction. His grades began slipping. He'd been an honors student before, and now he was barely passing. He was having trouble with relationships. I noticed his lifelong best friend wasn't in touch. I assumed it was because they attended different high schools. My son and I had always been able to talk, but I found him harder to communicate with. He was evasive and irritable. I attributed it to him being a moody teenager.

By March 2017, he was expelled from his high school. We transferred him to our district high school, nearby. He was ditching classes and bringing kids home in the middle of the day. We really didn't understand what was going wrong. He just wasn't himself.

He played baseball that summer—a healthy activity until a teammate supplied him with more marijuana. We eventually began to understand his behavioral changes were due to marijuana use, and we began searching his room for drug paraphernalia. There were items that looked like zip drives; they were high-potency THC vapes. We found drug items in tissue boxes, patio furniture cushions, and fence posts. Apples were disappearing. We came to understand he was using apples as bongs to smoke marijuana! He also used aluminum foil to burn the dabs made of waxy resin.

He became more and more morose. He was always tired. He said his joints hurt. His stomach hurt. We took him to his doctor. We were unable to be involved in the conversations. He had privacy because he was over 13. We started drug testing him. We would take away his phone or his video games when he was positive. He raged at us. He pounded on the front door so hard the metal dented. He yelled and accused anyone around him of strange, unrealistic conspiracies. It was hellacious. I didn't want him to be around his three younger sisters.

It was easy for him to access marijuana from kids at school. Eventually, we decided to homeschool him to try to keep him safe. However, with a smartphone, he could "order" his drugs … and have them delivered.

We continued to scour our property to intervene. We took his door off the hinges and tried to find his drugs. It became an arms race. He lied, stole, and hid his stash. We locked our bedroom door and office door and kept throwing away his marijuana.

In October 2018, he agreed to go to an outpatient program through the University of Colorado Anschutz, which specializes in substance abuse counseling and behavioral health, though he later told us he would cheat on his urine tests to look compliant. We started him at a new local high school. They were supportive, but it didn't last long. After meeting with the dean, our son dropped out.

The next crisis was COVID in March 2020. Our son was unhappy with our living situation and rules, so he moved in with a girlfriend, whose dad thought he was helping him out. He was there for approximately a year. We tried to stay in contact with him. We bought groceries and visited—that is, when they answered the door. He was holding down a job as a stock clerk at Walmart. His girlfriend eventually broke up with him, and he came back home. We could tell he was still using marijuana. We wanted to sleep at night and keep the peace to the best of our ability. So, we decided the safest choice was to have him live in our camper. This was heart-wrenching. He had shelter. He had heat. He had food. He had a family. But he was living apart from us ... he was in the driveway, but he may as well have been 100 miles away.

A miracle happened. A book arrived. It was written by Laura Stack, and this book changed our lives. She sent it to us at her own expense. I couldn't put it down. I was riveted. I was feeling validated about our experience with our son. I told my parents and in-laws about it. Finally, someone understood what we were going through, and yet, I was depleted and deeply saddened by the reality of what Laura's family had experienced.

After participating in witness testimony at the Colorado State Capitol, we realized we were "trying to sweep the ocean back with a broomstick." Many people with similar stories shared them publicly. That very night, we had a difficult conversation with our son. We calmly related what we had learned—the extent to which this addiction can damage people. We had seen much of it ourselves, but somehow, we thought we were unique, or in the minority. The shroud of silence was isolating. When we did reach out for help and support, there were many people who just didn't know what to say or do. "It's just weed . . . " was the general response.

The next step for our family was when we sent our 18-year-old son to an inpatient facility in Steamboat Springs, Colorado. I drove him there. I left him with strangers. I had dreamed of dropping him off at college; this was a far cry from that reality. We didn't know how long he'd be away. But we did know we wouldn't have contact with him for 10 days. Even in the darkest of times, we hadn't gone that long without speaking. He stayed six weeks. He turned 19 while he was at the treatment center. When we picked him up, he was "himself" again.

Now, our son is nearly 22 years old. He is gainfully employed full-time and attends college. He is busy collecting playing cards and snowboarding. I can't say he is "cured." Addiction isn't like that. But he has a chance. While he was under the influence of marijuana, he couldn't think straight or advocate for himself much. I am extremely grateful we had enough influence on him to go to treatment. I'm grateful he acquiesced. I'm grateful he did the hard work.

At the time, our health insurance denied our claim. They didn't recognize marijuana addiction as a qualification for treatment. We spent over $50,000 to help our son. That was just the cost of the inpatient treatment. This habit has an enormous cost to families. It is costing children their innocence and childhood. It is hurting siblings and parents. It is causing so much pain. It is robbing people of their right mind and their freedom.

CHAPTER 14:
Always Forgive Everyone and Spend Time with Those We Love

ON MARCH 27, 2019, our lives were forever changed. We were devastated by the untimely death of our second child at the young age of 18. Considering that marijuana is the drug directly responsible for killing my child, the drug that was in his blood when he died, I thought it was important to share our story in hopes of saving another family the heartache of losing their child to marijuana.

Aaron was an intelligent, handsome young man. He had a beautiful, compassionate, forgiving, self-sacrificing spirit, and quiet nature. He was accepting and loving of everyone. He had a quick wit and was always joking around with family and friends. As he said a few weeks prior to his death, "Mom, we must always forgive everyone and spend time with those we love." That was my Aaron; he was my precious, kind boy.

How Our Nightmare Began

When Aaron was 16 years old, a friend from school helped him obtain a job as a busboy at a restaurant in Fallston, Maryland. Aaron was so excited about his interview! With his dad's help, he typed up a résumé, dressed up in a suit, and obtained his first job. Little did I know this was the beginning of the end of Aaron's life.

The woman who recommended to the manager that Aaron be hired had a long criminal history. She had a plan to start a medical marijuana business. She worked at the restaurant as a waitress, along with her son, daughter, and stepson.

The mother knew Aaron was a bright student in the business program at Eastern Technical High School. He had dreams of becoming a certified management accountant. From all the information we learned after Aaron's death, we believe this family befriended and groomed Aaron to assist them with their criminal enterprise. They were making marijuana edibles and selling it through the restaurant. In addition, the restaurant workers who had medical marijuana cards sold high-potency THC honey, shatter, wax, and budder to the other younger kids working there.

We started seeing changes in Aaron's behavior a little over a year before his death. He had a new group of work friends and became secretive. He was always eager to go to work, avoided family activities, and became more aggressive and despondent. However, I did not wake up to the real changes until it was too late. One day, when I attempted to kiss his forehead while he was asleep on the family room couch, he jumped up and almost punched me in the face! I didn't understand why he was suddenly so paranoid and prone to anger.

I had to leave as I was running late to work, but I thought about his behavior that whole day. While discussing this with a coworker, they said Aaron was exhibiting all the signs of marijuana dependency, as their own son had struggled with this addiction in the past. The friend also informed me that driving under the influence of marijuana was worse than drunk driving. By the time I got home that night, around 9:00 p.m., Aaron was already at work.

The Night Aaron Died

Aaron never came home the night of March 27, 2019. His marijuana impairment and addiction, along with his THC-induced paranoid delusions, caused him to veer off the road on his way home and crash into the woods off I-95. While he was waiting for his friend to pick him up, according to reports, Aaron then got out of his car and walked onto I-95, where he was run over and killed by another driver. The driver who hit him was 27 years old, with a previous history of marijuana possession and DUI while impaired by a controlled substance. A witness who saw my son at the scene said he appeared totally lost and confused, not in his right mind, and seemed to not know what he was doing. I know Aaron wouldn't have killed himself if he hadn't been astronomically high from THC. He had no intention of dying by suicide.

Based on the investigative reports we obtained, and despite his history, the police who responded to the accident scene never tested the 27-year-old for impairment of any kind. In addition, despite numerous statements in the police report of the strong odor of marijuana coming from Aaron's car, they called his manner of death a suicide, even though they never tested his blood for THC.

One week after Aaron's death, we were able to pick up his belongings from the towing company's lot, where his totaled car was held. The smell of marijuana was still so overpowering we had to take turns retrieving Aaron's possessions from his car. We called the medical examiner's office to find out the results of the toxicology report. Surprisingly, the toxicology report did not include the results for marijuana testing. We described the strong smell of marijuana coming from Aaron's car and pressed for the retesting of Aaron's blood for THC. As we expected, the results were quite high for

THC. From sharing his results with marijuana experts, we learned Aaron was "acutely intoxicated + long-term use." This report confirmed his THC addiction and THC impairment the night he died.

My daughter knew about his use before we did.

While talking with my daughter, I found out she had known of Aaron's marijuana use but did not inform us because of what she had been taught at school. She attended Perry Hall High School, where the school, without the informed consent of parents, had a guest speaker at an assembly for the science students. The guest speaker was a bone marrow transplant patient who was using medical marijuana. The speaker was invited to inform the teens of the benefits of this federally illicit, Schedule I drug. The patient apparently informed the teens that marijuana is just an herb from an ancient plant that helped ease her pain, anxiety, and depression. As a nurse, I was astonished at this, since my cancer patients who use marijuana have much worse outcomes than those who are drug-free.

I was shocked that the school would allow the marijuana industry into our schools. The ramifications of this misinformation led to the death of my son. I believe if my daughter and son had been provided with the truth about the risks of high-THC products and had not been fed blatant lies about marijuana, my son would still be alive today!

CHAPTER 15

Ryan's Unbreakable Spirit and Perseverance

RYAN, OUR YOUNGEST SON, arrived three years after his brother, in April 2000. He completed our family of four and was a calm, cheerful, and funny child. His early years were active and happy, revolving around his love of baseball. Ryan excelled in high school, was never the "partying type," and jokingly said he didn't want a girlfriend because they were "too much drama." Ryan always stayed focused and responsible, and he got a scholarship to a community college where he planned to go before transferring to a university to study finance.

Ryan's first experience with weed was a vape (or wax) pen in February of his senior year. He said it was social and it really didn't "do anything for him." That summer, after graduation, he started using marijuana more frequently, ultimately becoming addicted. By August, when his college classes started, he was using THC every day but hiding it well. I started to notice something was different about him as he suddenly seemed overconfident and spent an excessive amount of time gaming.

An event in September 2018 marked the end of life as we knew it; we had no idea what we soon would be facing. Our once happy and stable family would change forever—and at the core of its destruction was high-potency THC.

Confused and Crying:
*"I really f***ed up."*

I remember this life-changing moment like it was yesterday, even though it happened more than five years ago. Our confident, happy-go-lucky son suddenly was in tears and said, "Mom, Dad … I really f***ed up." He began talking very slowly, and his speech was labored as he shared these concerns: "I'm so behind in school. I can't catch up. I can't do my accelerated class. I'm going to lose my scholarship. I'm scared about my new job. I don't think I can go to my training at work. I won't have money for my car payment. I don't want to move out and live on campus next year. I don't know what kind of job I will get after college. I don't think I can even finish college." *Whoa!*

We thought this was anxiety, but in the next few days, he said he was having trouble sleeping and his mind would not stop worrying. I told him things would be okay and encouraged him to go on his previously planned fall break trip to the lake with his brother and some friends. I thought nature would help him reset and relax and give him a new perspective on things. Looking back now, I realize the trip was a bad idea.

Doom and Gloom:
"It was cold. It was rainy. Something happened."

He hesitantly left for the trip on Thursday morning, and when he returned Sunday night, I asked him if he felt any better. He said he felt worse and there was something he needed to tell us. He had a blank stare on his face and struggled to find the words to explain what was going on. All he said, over and over, was it was cold and rainy, and something had happened. He kept repeating those words using fragments instead of full sentences. I asked him if he did any drugs while he was there, and he said he didn't. But he later told us he vaped THC and drank some alcohol. I thought maybe the THC was laced with something because to my knowledge, marijuana couldn't have that type of effect.

Symptoms and Psychosis:
"This is the best I've felt in a long time!"

The next week was a blur. Ryan was trying to study but couldn't concentrate or retain any information. He started getting very depressed and had trouble making simple decisions, from what clothes to wear to what to eat. We met with two therapists that week. The first one asked Ryan if he smoked weed. "Ya, a little," he said. I told her he just used it occasionally, and I didn't want to focus on that. I had no idea he was using much more heavily than he was telling us, and the weed he was using was 80–90 percent THC. The therapist told us to sell his car, drop his classes, and find a drug rehab center ASAP! At that point, I had zero dots connected and thought this advice was extreme, unsympathetic, and unrealistic.

Next, we went to a psychiatrist, who told us Ryan had all the classic symptoms of depression and anxiety. To minimize stress, we decided it would be best to have Ryan withdraw from his classes and quit his job. That same week, he was thinking about suicide, so we took him to a crisis center. He could barely fill out the intake form, but after an extensive interview, they told him because he had such a strong family support system, it was safe for him to return home under our close watch. Upon hearing this, Ryan's doctor prescribed a low-dose antidepressant.

Ryan's symptoms included:

- anxiety/nervousness
- delusionsinability to focus, concentrate, or memorize
- difficulty finishing sentences
- worry about the future
- hot and cold flashes
- insomnia and racing thoughts
- hopelessness/catastrophizing
- suicidal thoughts
- no hygiene
- negative thinking
- slowed speech

Within four days on the antidepressant, Ryan said, "Mom, this is the best I've felt in a long time!" I was very relieved our son could now complete sentences and seemed more like his old self. My folks offered to take Ryan with them to the mountains for a few days to relax. He went with them; however, my folks cut the trip short and told us something was wrong, saying Ryan was driving and talking fast and seemed irrational. Once home, he was hyper, not listening, vaping excessively, and had no impulse control. The doctor said to stop the medication immediately, and because of this manic reaction, diagnosed Ryan with bipolar disorder and ordered mood stabilizers for him.

Depression and Despair:
"I don't want to heal."

Our family has no genetic predisposition for bipolar disorder, and I found it frightening that the antidepressant could cause such a shift in personality. We then discovered Ryan had been using weed during that time. Once he stopped using it, he started to get depressed again. In early December, he had to have his wisdom teeth extracted. I told him I had made him a green smoothie to help him heal, and he said, "I don't want to heal." That was so heartbreaking to hear. Within a week, he started to feel better, but then the cycle repeated. He vaped nicotine and THC, spent irresponsibly, lied, ate junk food, drank energy drinks, and stayed up all night gaming and gambling. His demeanor became flippant, aloof, and forgetful. One night, he vaped so much he got sick and slept on the bathroom floor. Upon waking, he threw away all his "stash" and said he was quitting for good.

Mistrust and Fear:
"What's wrong with me?"

The next four years were a roller-coaster loop of these same cycles, but the manic episodes had more devastating consequences. Ryan saw therapists and counselors who told us how much better he was doing. Then, they would see his manic cycle, and after several months, they told us Ryan needed a higher level of care, and our son was addicted to THC. I had only ever heard weed was not addictive, so I was confused.

In 2020, we enrolled Ryan in a partial hospitalization program (PHP). COVID protocols allowed him to make up missed classes, so he was able to get his associate degree. While he managed to hold down a food delivery job, it unfortunately gave him the freedom and resources to go to dispensaries. That year, he totaled his car, and in one night of gaming, racked up more than $12,000 in credit card debt. We caught him stealing our cash and credit cards, and we thought, *Who is this young man we once called our son?* After each relapse, he regretted his past behaviors and was scared to make any decisions. We were all very frustrated, and Ryan would always say, "I don't know why I keep making these same bad choices. What's wrong with me?"

His next therapist helped him understand he needed to be in a residential treatment center. She told him if he didn't go, these cycles would continue, and he would end up 1) in jail, 2) institutionalized, or 3) dead.

Thankfully, Ryan agreed, and we had an advocate help us find a dual diagnosis center that specialized in bipolar disorder and addiction. It was very difficult, and my husband accompanied Ryan on a flight across the country to the facility where he would stay from September through December 2022.

It was a tough start, but within two weeks, Ryan was doing well and was even named "Peer Leader." The transition plan for his return home was to first move into a sober living facility an hour and a half from our home. However, upon his release, Ryan walked into a gas station and bought a Delta-8 vape he used on the way to the airport. I knew the minute we met him outside of security, he seemed "off." The next day, I gave him a drug test, and it was positive for THC. I was in disbelief and wondered if the sober living facility would even take him. He apologized, telling us he didn't know what came over him. As expected, he had an episode of depression.

Destruction and Dismay:
"Can you come help?"

From January through May 2023, Ryan was in another PHP, but the cycles repeated, and he relapsed each month. The house manager was very compassionate and understanding, providing support and therapy. But that support came to an end in May when Ryan's relapse spiraled out of control. This time, Ryan was told he could no longer stay.

Ryan packed up his belongings, got into his car, and started randomly driving hundreds of miles around the state. I barely slept, worried sick, as I tracked his phone almost every minute. We knew he would run out of gas eventually, as he had no money, and his credit card was at its limit.

Finally, he texted us and asked if we could help him because he needed gas. We told him, "No," and said the only way we would come to help was if he agreed to go back into treatment. He agreed, so we set off to get him. When we arrived, Ryan told us his car was a couple of miles down the road in a tow truck lot! The previous night, he was driving while high and fell asleep at the wheel. He later told us he vaguely remembered cars flashing their lights and honking at him. At 2 a.m., he ended up driving across oncoming lanes into a ditch and passed out until the police woke him around 5 a.m. Apparently, the weed wore off because he didn't get arrested, and he wasn't even given a sobriety test.

As we took everything out of his totaled car, I found empty THC cartridges and gummy wrappers among junk food and other garbage. He had always been neat, organized, and very respectful of his things, so seeing this was symbolic of what a mess his life had become. We then called a recommended rehab center, but after a brief interview, they told us his admittance was denied because his addiction was "only" weed.

Lost and Broken:
"I'm never going back to residential ... I'd rather be homeless."

Ryan could not come back home, but we had no idea where to take him. The manager from his previous house was amazing and helped us find another treatment center. After a few calls, we were in touch with a wonderful counselor who told us his team could meet with us first thing in the morning. However, as we started to make the drive, Ryan told us he would never go back to another residential center and would rather be homeless. Our hearts sank, and my husband broke down and had to pull off the road to compose himself. We thought this might be the end of the line for our son as we could not force him into treatment against his will.

The next morning, we met with therapists and were given a tour of the facility. Ryan smiled a bit when he saw they had a softball league, but when it was time for him to commit, Ryan refused. He said to just drop him off on the curb. So, we gave him his duffel bag and phone, but he had no money, no job, and no car. This was one of the hardest things we have ever done. As we drove away, we were sobbing, not knowing if this was the right thing to do, or if this might be the last time that we would see our son. Within an hour, Ryan texted us and let us know he had decided to check himself into the center. This gave us temporary relief, and his counselor assured us he would be safe there.

From late May through October, Ryan thrived and remained sober. He was still having his typical cycles but was working on managing and recognizing his manic episodes. He also had a cognitive brain test that stated bipolar disorder was inconclusive, but it did confirm cannabis use disorder (CUD).

By October, Ryan had been accepted into a sober living house and had a new job. He was reenrolled in a course from the university and had a plan for continuing care, including an intensive outpatient program (IOP). He purchased an older, reliable car for work and rehab meetings. All the pieces were in place for his future success. As we finished helping him move, we noticed he seemed a little upbeat, but we just thought he was excited about this next phase of his recovery. (Clearly, I need to learn to trust my gut instincts better.)

Frustration and Surprise:
"I've been off my meds for three weeks."

In the next two weeks, Ryan had another relapse that jeopardized everything he had just worked so hard to achieve. One night, at 2 a.m., after intercepting his paycheck, which was for his rent, he drove for over an hour to a casino and gambled away the entire amount. He wasn't going to his job or to meetings, and we felt it was just a matter of time before he was homeless.

When Ryan finally snapped out of it, he couldn't believe the havoc he had caused. Depression set in, and he stayed in bed for days and barely ate. Then, he told me he hadn't been taking his meds for the prior three weeks! I was so scared, shocked, and upset. I made an emergency appointment with his doctor.

We were always told it would be very dangerous to stop his medications "cold turkey," and that tapering should be done only in a hospital under close observation. Whenever I questioned if his meds could be responsible for his mood swings, I was told no. It was not until this current doctor's visit that we got clarity. We again asked if the meds could be causing these episodes, and she said, "Absolutely!" This made us hopeful, but furious. Since he had no side effects or adverse reactions to stopping his meds, we decided to see how he would do without them.

Stopping meds became a turning point in Ryan's life. At first, he had a depressed cycle, but then ... nothing. The holidays came and went, and I held my breath waiting for any signs of manic or depressed behavior, but he remained balanced.

Healing and Hope:
"I feel dull, but it's probably because I'm used to such extreme highs and lows."

Our family has been in crisis mode for so long that writing Ryan's story feels like a dream. I have such respect and admiration for Laura Stack. It was her heart-wrenching, informative book that opened my eyes, made me trust my gut, inspired me to do more research, and gave me the courage to stand up to the medical establishment with enough confidence to challenge their advice and say, "He is staying off the medication. We believe his psychosis was cannabis-induced. The mood stabilizers kept him in a manic and depressed cycle. We want to allow his brain to heal naturally to see what his baseline mood looks like."

As of this writing, Ryan is three months sober and hasn't been on medication for three and a half months. At first, Ryan said he felt a little "dull," but he understands that compared to his life before, which was filled with such extreme highs and lows, it will take some time for his dopamine levels to return to normal. He is still in the sober living house and working steadily to save money to repay debts. He sees a therapist once a week and staying sober is his number one priority. Ryan is finding that without mania, he no longer has the cravings or impulsivity he used to have. High-potency THC caused Ryan's initial psychotic break with bipolar-like symptoms, but the mood-stabilizing meds he was on, combined with the continued THC use, caused the repeating cycles.

Everything Ryan experienced needed to happen to give him the information and tools to be successful in his recovery. He has been through the 12-step program, has a community of support, and appreciates having a patient, loving family. He is humble and has deeper compassion for what an addicted person goes through.

Ryan is one of the lucky ones, and it is with gratitude I can write and share our story in hopes it can help others gain insight and understanding in a world where so little information exists about the dangers of THC.

Heartbroken and Helpless:
"It's positive for THC."

Apparently, I was premature in announcing our hoped-for happy ending. Two weeks after this story was finalized, Ryan began exhibiting signs of mania again. We brought it to his attention, and he assured us he was not having any cravings and was doing great. He said he was meeting new friends and starting to have a social life again, which is why he seemed so upbeat. We gave him the benefit of the doubt as he had been doing so well. However, he also was not doing the things he was supposed to be very careful about—such as limiting caffeine consumption, managing nicotine vaping, maintaining consistent sleep, and controlling his involvement in social media. Then, we found out he had missed his therapy appointment and went to a casino and blew all his rent money. These behaviors and other red flags led us to the decision to drive 90 miles to his workplace on a Friday night, talk to him, and give him a drug test.

We knew something was wrong as soon as he walked out of the door. He did not make eye contact with us and went straight to his car. His demeanor was totally different from the week prior. We asked him to get in the car with us, and we drove to a convenience store so he could do the test. It was a long five-minute wait, and Ryan sat quietly in the back seat. When I pulled off the test strip, it showed he was positive for THC. I think we knew what the result would be, but we were still holding out hope it might be negative.

We shared our disappointment and told him we would be taking his car keys, per the contract he signed previously. He remained silent, not providing any excuses or reasons for his relapse. We knew it would be a matter of time before his house tested him, and then he would have to find a new place to live. After we left, we texted him words of encouragement, telling him it wasn't too late to turn things around, get back on track, and when he is ready, we will be there for him. But he went "radio silent" and turned off his location. The only way we know he is okay is by checking his bank account, which is repeatedly being overdrawn.

Now, we wait. At some point, Ryan will snap out of this cycle and stop using THC. Then, depression will set in. This story is ongoing, and all we can do is learn from the past. We hope we can find a doctor who can offer a solution that will finally help our son get his life back. It is an agonizing wait.

CHAPTER 16:

Our Family's First Nightmare: How Is This Happening?

BEFORE I BEGIN MY STORY, I'd like whoever is reading this to know the only way we made it through this ordeal was with our Lord and Savior Jesus Christ. Without Him, I do not know where we would be, but I do know that His mercy and His grace is what helped us through this whole scary ordeal. We had a prayer chain going from the beginning. We know the power of all the prayers constantly flowing helped us as well. We give all the glory to God.

Lou is our youngest daughter, born in April 2001. We had two other daughters, a 12-year-old and an 8-year-old, so technically we were done, or so we thought, but God had other plans. Lou was a very happy baby. She met all her milestones in a timely fashion and was always smiling. She was very outgoing, especially because she had two sisters to keep up with.

We experienced some devastation in her early years. My mother passed away on Christmas Eve in 2007. She lived with us at one time and was a big part of all our lives, and a year and a half later, my husband and I were rear-ended by a very intoxicated 23-year-old. My husband was badly injured. We were told he was going to be paralyzed from the neck down. Then we were told it would be from the waist down. After multiple surgeries and months of rehabilitation, and a visit from an angel, he is walking and working and doing well.

Through all of this, Lou was trying to navigate middle school, and unfortunately, she was somewhat bullied. She was a late bloomer, tiny with a smaller chest than her peers. She hated school, and even though she was getting amazing grades and had teachers who loved her, she just couldn't take it. We ended up homeschooling for a year, which was okay but still had its challenges. Now she was home all the time and didn't have much outside communication with her remaining friends. Out of sight, out of mind.

We ended up moving to the neighboring town, and Lou went back to public school, repeating the eighth grade. Well, it was wonderful. She made some good friends, loved her teachers, and got into sports. She really blossomed. She was a year older than most of her peers, which bothered her a bit; however, she kept that under wraps for some time. Lou started dating a sweet boy who worshipped the ground she walked on. They were exclusive for almost two years. In her sophomore year, they broke up and she was devastated. She kept her grades up, was in a couple of AP classes, had a consistent 4.0 GPA, and still hung out with some decent girls and boys.

Lou started seeing this new boy she had known since eighth grade. He was nice to her, but he smoked a lot of weed. We knew she had been smoking a little with a couple of friends, and of course, we were like all the other parents who say, "It's just pot," not knowing how strong and different it was. The summer of 2018, before her junior year, she seemed different. She had been in volleyball for the first two years of high school and had established a great spot on her team. She was supposed to keep practicing and preparing for the tryouts but wasn't. We started noticing she wasn't sleeping much. She was snappy. She wasn't keeping her room picked up. All she wanted to do was hang out with this guy and his friends and get high.

Up until this year, she and I had a good relationship. We went to lunch and got our toenails done together. We watched movies and just really enjoyed each other. She was a good girl. She did what she knew she needed to do and listened to us. Now, however, she was just different.

The day before the first day of school was the volleyball tryouts. Unfortunately, there were two new coaches. They didn't know anything about the team or the kids, not like the past two, who really had a good rapport with all the girls. Unfortunately, she got cut. A new freshman got her spot. She was beyond devastated. I have never in my life seen her like this. I was waiting for her to come out after tryouts, and she came to the car like a wild animal. She told me to come into the coaches' office. By the time I got in there, she was freaking out—yelling, crying, begging, and sobbing—not herself at all. I apologized to the coaches; I told them this was not my daughter. The rest of that day was pretty much a mess. All she wanted to do was go over to her druggy boyfriend's house and go kayaking. Of course, now I know, it was to get high and forget, to numb herself.

The next day was the first day of school. She barely slept the night before. She was also vaping nicotine during this time. She got up after maybe four hours of sleep and got ready, and I drove her to school. She was still not herself. I was very concerned. She looked different. It's hard to explain, but she had a strange smirk. Lou texted one of her sisters from school, saying very weird things. Her sister in turn sent me screenshots of what she was saying. She was about to get on a flight for work, so she called me and said, "Mom, you need to go get her." I went into my husband's office and told him what was going on. Our oldest daughter was at home at the time, as she was in nursing school, and we all jumped in the car and went to the high school and picked her up. She was a mess, and she was saying things that made no sense at all. She was telling us her first boyfriend, the one she was with for so long, had raped her all through their relationship. I am her mom and knew this was not true at all. She was talking about the job she had, which was babysitting for this little boy, and she was saying the father was inappropriate with her, which I also knew was not true.

We ended up taking her to the hospital, where she spent the night in the psychiatric unit's holding tank, so to speak, and then they transferred her to a different hospital the next day. By the time all was said and done during the intake, she told the doctor and nurses she was raped by a guard at the last hospital, which again, I knew wasn't true. So now they sent us to another hospital, where she had to have a rape test done, and the police had to be called, and the police had to go to the other hospital and look at the surveillance camera, which showed her sleeping pretty much the entire time she was there.

After that, we went back to the psychiatric hospital, where she stayed for a few days, and in plain English was completely delusional. She saw things on the wall, which she said were the three wisemen watching her. She gave everything and anything meaning. She threatened her dad and me by saying she was going to defecate in a paper bag if we didn't take her out of the hospital, and when we told her she had to stay there, she pulled her pants down and defecated in a paper bag. I was so scared. She was running around in this room like a caged animal. Then they told us we had to leave. She clung to my husband's leg, crying, "Please don't leave!" With the devastation and heartbreak and everything that goes along with that, leaving her was horrific.

After her being there for a few days, they transferred her to Yale New Haven Hospital, where they did a lot of different tests, CAT scans, MRIs, brain scans, you name it. Earlier in the year, in January of 2018, she caught mononucleosis. We understand this, along with the marijuana, more than likely helped her psychosis and mania come to life, due to her blood-brain barrier being compromised. They were checking every inch of her body to see what was causing this, even though I knew what caused it. They just didn't believe marijuana could be the cause of this. She was still completely out of her mind while we were there, still not sleeping, talking about a baby down the hallway that was crying and saying it was her baby and why weren't we bringing her baby to breastfeed—lots of weird, weird, weird things.

After nine days of being in that hospital, they transferred her over to Yale New Haven's psychiatric unit. She was there for two weeks. I didn't go home for those two weeks. I stayed in a hotel where it's less expensive for people whose loved ones are in the hospitals in the area. I couldn't go home. I couldn't leave my baby an hour away from me; I needed to be close. This was before COVID, so I was able to see her every single day. They let me come in during breakfast, lunch, and dinner. I was very fortunate with this. They were trying all different medications to bring her back to her "baseline," as they called it, and after two weeks they sent her home. She was still not herself and shouldn't have come home. She continued assigning inanimate objects with real-life functions. For example, the rocks near our house all played roles—the big one was the daddy rock, and it was there to protect the other rocks, which were the mommy and baby rocks.

She was in an intensive outpatient program (IOP) three days a week. The fourth day of being home, she was in the IOP when she stood up and said something off the wall, so they called me and said she needed to go back to the hospital. They allowed all of us to go pick her up and drive her back to Yale New Haven, and she was there for six more weeks until she was finally able to come home.

She was on many different medications, and she was childlike. By that I mean she was now 18 years old, but some days she seemed to be 5 or 8 years old; she couldn't even open a cream cheese package. (By the way, we had obtained conservatorship because we were afraid if something happened again and she was 18, we wouldn't be able to help.) She would ask me things like, "What kind of sprinkles should I get on my ice cream cone?" She was like a little child, and it was the scariest, most horrible thing to go through for all of us. We were so afraid this was it.

I wouldn't allow this kind of thinking, and I prayed fervently. Over the next eight months, she had a psychiatrist for medication, and a therapist.

She also went back to the IOP, which was very helpful, and she made a sweet friend there. This helped her a lot in being able to become social again. She couldn't go back to school; it was too overwhelming, and she had missed too much. Also, her "friends" completely ditched her, only a couple were still her friends. She was depressed over this. Thankfully, she has a very loving family, and we all rallied around her and kept her grounded. We played games; we watched movies; we painted birdhouses; we built puzzles; and we went on countless walks.

Eventually the psychiatrist started lowering her medication very slowly, weaning her off completely, and she has never gone back into psychosis because she has never smoked marijuana again. She is medication-free. She is drug-free. She is nicotine-free. She is amazing! She got her GED and still had a 4.0. She is now 22 years old and married a man she was with for four years while he was in the Marines. She is about to enter a nursing program. We are so proud of her. She went through so much and came out with God on the other side, better than ever.

CHAPTER 17:

Our Family's Second Nightmare: Please, God, Not Again!

OUR SECOND JOURNEY with cannabis-induced psychosis (CIP) was with our middle adult daughter, Sara, born in 1993. She was very smart; she was talking in almost complete sentences by the time she was 20 months old. It was amazing, and even her doctor was shocked. At one of her appointments he said, "Can you say Harvard?" The nurse and I giggled because we knew exactly what he was saying. From that point on, her development was normal. She was in awe of her sister who was three and a half years older. Sara was her sidekick and wanted to be with her all the time. By the time Sara was 15, she had a full-time job and was very driven by saving money and learning as much as possible. When she was 16, she became a manager at that same job, and she would go to work and do schoolwork while she was there. Of course, by high school, she was drinking and partying like a lot of the kids did and still do these days. At times, she did these things a little bit too much. She was very strong-willed and thought she knew more than her dad and me. She made it through high school and graduated with amazing grades. She went to college for four years and graduated *magna cum laude* with a degree in communications and went to work for NBC.

At this time, she'd had a boyfriend for almost seven years. They went to high school together and moved in together when she started her first job. After some time, they realized it wasn't going to work out, especially because he was a habitual marijuana smoker, and she didn't care for it much. She moved back home for a short time and then ended up getting her own apartment. All this time, she was saving money and still partying, but she mainly drank alcohol. Most of her friends were just "party friends." She ended up meeting this guy at a new job. They worked together, and he was very nice to her in the beginning. He moved in with her, even though we told her it wasn't a good idea. Throughout the next couple of years, he was very verbally abusive. Unfortunately, she didn't share with us just how bad it was. When their lease was finally up, she moved back home, and they slowly broke up. It was really a blessing in disguise, even though she felt sad because they shared what they call a "trauma bond."

Sara started seeing someone who was younger than her. He was fun and not like the horrible last guy. However, he was a habitual marijuana smoker as were all his friends. She started smoking because she was going through some depression and had some anxiety. These new friends convinced her weed was helpful, even though she never really liked it. She started to seem different to all of us. She was crying a lot, but sometimes she was just super happy. She was either up or down. I remember having a conversation with her and telling her it's probably not a good idea for her to continue smoking because we'd noticed a change, and she didn't seem like our daughter. She agreed, but she kept doing it.

Fast-forward to November 2020 when she was 27 years old. On Thanksgiving Day, she had a big argument with her dad, which caused her to break down hysterically crying. She felt like she might be suffering from PTSD because of the abuse she had endured with her ex. Looking back to this moment, she had entered psychosis, but we all thought she was going through a deep depression. Her actions started to get more erratic. She was extremely sad but also quick to anger. She and a girlfriend went to Florida for New Year's. She decided to continue smoking, and unfortunately, she did cocaine in a bar with strangers. While she was in Florida, she impulsively decided to go out with a realtor and buy a condo in Miami. We begged her not to, but she said she was just going to live there for a short period of time, and then she was going to rent it so she could make money. When she moved to Florida, she was already in psychosis, but we didn't realize it at the time. Sara was also manic. She was not sleeping and was barely eating. She was still working her virtual job. It was surreal to us she could function somewhat normally when needed.

From February until August, her behavior was all over the map. She destroyed her condo—painted the walls and ripped up the floors. She thought she was being creative. She thought she was basically God. She was dabbling in weird rituals with crystals, tarot cards, and things she knew we were totally against. She said she was going to be a singer, star in a Netflix series, and was going to be making $1 million by the end of the year. She was exhibiting what's called "grandiose behavior." Unfortunately, everything she did, she posted on her Instagram livestream. Anyone who knew her from childhood—my friends, her friends, her coworkers, etc.—could watch her extremely destructive behavior. The expression on her face was so weird; it was as if she were possessed. Everything she talked about made no sense at all. She drove like she was a speed racer, putting so many people, including herself, in danger. In her live videos, she did things that scared everyone who cared about her. She made friends with the homeless people on the streets and gave them excessive amounts of money. She allowed three random boys in their early 20s to stay in her apartment for a couple of days because they were on vacation and didn't have anywhere to stay. She put herself in such unimaginably scary situations.

We all are so thankful to God she is still here. All this behavior happened because of the high-potency THC she was doing with these people. We had her taken to a hospital in an ambulance when she was visiting us. Of course, they kept her for only a day and sent her home because she wasn't an imminent danger to herself or others. She needed help, but we couldn't get it.

Finally, in August 2021, at the age of 28, Sara had a breakdown and went to her older sister's apartment on Long Island. Her sister's partner, who is a psychiatric nurse, talked her into going to the hospital and getting assessed. She ended up getting admitted and was transferred to a psychiatric hospital. Sara wouldn't stay there because she knew somebody who worked there. At the second hospital, our ability to talk to the doctors changed daily depending on how she felt about us. It was a control thing. The doctor we spoke to said she was going to be released because she seemed fine, and she was refusing medication. While on the phone with the doctor, my husband and I explained what we had been through with Sara, and the doctor said he was going to provoke her to get an atypical response like the ones we were seeing. The doctor proceeded to discuss with her what we discussed with him, and she went berserk. They gave her medicine to help her sleep.

The next morning, she called and spoke to her father briefly. Then she proceeded to call me. She said she was done with me and was never going to talk to me or see me again. I hung up. I quickly called the hospital to speak to a nurse or a doctor, but she had already revoked our rights. We didn't know if she was still there or had left the hospital. Out of the blue, she finally called and informed us she was going to be in front of a judge (via Zoom) to see if he would let her leave the facility. She said we couldn't attend because the doctor said there could be only one person with her. She chose her lovely boyfriend to be in this court hearing. Our hands were tied. There was absolutely nothing we could do.

I prayed for God to please not allow her release. After the hearing she called me and said her boyfriend really pulled through for her. The judge released her into his care. Every time we spoke to her was like walking on eggshells. We never wanted to say anything too harsh because we did not want her to run the other way. When I hung up the phone that day, I went to my husband, broke down, and said, "Our judicial system sucks. I cannot believe this judge is letting our precious child go with this disgusting person who has no regard for her." I went outside and started screaming at the top of my lungs. I was yelling at God and saying, "What did I do? Why are you doing this to us, to me?" Minutes later, I was sobbing uncontrollably and apologizing to God because I knew He was not doing anything to me. He was trying to help keep the enemy away and trying to make this terrible situation work for our good.

Well, let me tell you how good God is. The next day, my daughter called to let us know her boyfriend was picking her up from the facility, and they were going to go back to her apartment in Miami. I was an emotional mess, barely sleeping and praying all the time. About an hour and a half after the call from her, she called me through FaceTime. This was the first time in a long eight months I got to see my daughter's face—her normal, beautiful face. She told me she was having some clarity! I was so elated that it was very difficult to contain myself. She and I spoke for a few minutes, and she said she really wanted to see us but was three hours away, and she didn't know if it was going to work. Her dad and I were about to drive to her; however, her stupid boyfriend said they had to hurry up and get to their flight. He convinced her we were going to manipulate her and persuade her not to go back to Florida with him. We ended up not being able to see her. She got on that flight and went back to Florida.

Her boyfriend had a habit of, as he called it, "going off the grid." This is where he would turn off his cell phone, and he would disappear for unknown periods of time. He said he needed to regroup, which meant doing more drugs. For the next two weeks, she and I talked through FaceTime every single day for hours on end. I barely showered because I just stayed on the phone with her, and we laughed, and cried, and talked. She wanted to come home. We got her a ticket on August 28, 2021, and she came home! She was free from psychosis after eight months of CIP, and she has been free from drugs ever since. All the glory goes to God! I cannot say that enough. I pray all day every day! I will never, ever stop praying. I pray not just for my family but for all the people out there who are hurting and going through even a pinch of what we experienced. It was a nightmare. John 16:33 says, "These things I have spoken unto you, that in me ye might have peace. In the world ye shall have tribulation: but be of good cheer; I have overcome the world." God be with us.

CHAPTER 18:

A Battle for Sanity

IN 2008, OUR SON WAS BEGINNING his senior year in high school when a diagnosis of bipolar schizoaffective disorder blindsided our family. We know now, from our son's admission, his mental illness was triggered two years earlier by using highly potent marijuana. Our story—his story—is ultimately one of faith and hope.

Our faith provided insight and strength during the most challenging seasons of his life. We have been on this journey through the valley of mental illness for 16 years now and have wrestled with God over this question. Why would God, who loves us and loves our family, give us such a devastating diagnosis just as our handsome, loving, smart, and wonderful son was beginning a life full of promise? What we have learned is God did NOT give us this struggle and this illness; it is simply the result of brokenness in a broken world.

In her book *Stand: Rising Up Against the Darkness, Temptation, and Persecution*, Marian Jordan Ellis says a "Red Sea" moment is "to believe God even when facing heartbreak." She provides strategies to maintain peace in the storm. These are the strategies that have given us strength in our journey. During these Red Sea moments, we know God's word says:

- Plant your feet.
- Fix your heart.
- Physically reflect the faith in your heart.

We add from our experience that clinging to God's promises restores our strength and hope.

God's word in Exodus 14:14 says the Lord will fight for you, and you need only to be still. How many times has God fought for our family on this journey? We have kept a journal to document our journey through the valley of the shadow of insanity. This journey includes 16 hospitalizations and multiple life-threatening situations. What is our testimony? God was with us through it all. His word says in Deuteronomy 31:8: "The Lord himself goes before you and will be with you; he will never leave you nor forsake you. Do not be afraid; do not be discouraged."

God woke us up at just the right time to see something we needed to see at that instant. He sent the perfect person—an angel—whom we needed at that exact moment. We found that journaling during the dark times sustained us. Excerpts from our journal documenting the initial years and multiple relapses share our deepest thoughts during these dark nights of the soul.

August 2008

A Love Letter to My Son

Faith and love guide one family through suffering to hope.

My son, the memories of you flow through my very being. From the moment I could feel you tickling my womb with your perfectly formed arms and legs, I loved you. Even before you existed, Psalm 139:16 says all the days ordained for you were in your book before any of those days even happened.

As you grew, we loved you more. Those dark brown eyes of yours pierce my heart. Your wit and your sweet kindness to all are so pure and precious. I now cling to the joy and laughter of your childhood and our hopes and dreams for your future. A beautiful child grew into a handsome, strong, good young man with a great heart. God ordained your days to have great joy and is with you in your affliction and suffering. Psalm 139: 13-14 says God created you and knitted you together and you are fearfully and wonderfully made.

How was your suffering a part of God's plan for your life? How could He have knit together confusion and darkness in your mind? I cannot believe this darkness is from God, but I can believe God will deliver us from darkness. That is His promise if we believe.

Watching you suffer is so incredibly hard. I cannot do this hard work for you. I cannot stop it. I cannot help you with this. I cannot fix it. I would gladly change places with you, so you don't suffer. But it is your journey. Only you can choose to walk through this valley. All I can do is believe, with God's help, you will make it to the other side.

I don't understand why you must suffer with this anguish; all I know is God doesn't waste pain. He does, however, with our permission, use it, channel it, and direct our path toward others who are suffering. He knows those who are suffering give hope to others still trapped in darkness and anguish. I know, somehow, God will use your journey—our journey—to touch other lives and provide them with hope and safe passage to their recoveries.

Relapse 2012

Watching him slip away and succumb to the darkness of the valley of the shadow of insanity is terrifying for us; think how much more terrifying it is for our son. Like Charlie in Daniel Keyes's *Flowers for Algernon*, during the last 18 months our son has had the opportunity to realize his remarkable potential, gifts, and talents, only to be stolen away again. Those who love him struggle to keep him from falling over the cliff, gripping more tightly as, inch by inch, he keeps slipping. Our heels dig into the ground, plowing a trench, as the weight of the illness pulls him further over the cliff toward the valley. His eyes have lost their brightness as he struggles to understand what is happening to him. The rope burns our hands as it slips a little more each day; our arms are cramped, and our hearts are breaking.

Lord, give us strength today, and help our son know he can trust us, his doctor, and the medications. We pray our voices, the doctor's voice, and his dream of graduating with a welding degree will be a bright light in this darkness, like a foothold to give him the strength to pull himself back to reality. In Jesus's name, Amen.

Relapse 2015

The call, the feeling in my gut, my throat constricting, knowing we are embarking again on the terrifying journey of relapse. Why are we stepping in now when we have set clear boundaries and let consequences play out? Now, this time, it is different. Now it's life-threatening; now it's out of state. No one else in this world will look for our son.

Relapse 2017

"I love you, but I am no longer afraid to tell you I am no longer a part of this family" is the text I read in the early morning hours in May 2017.

Lord, be with us as we go down this terrifying journey again. Help us to find our son. Again, it's life-threatening; again, our son relapsed out of state, and this time, out of the country. We are the only ones between our son and a lifetime of homelessness and dying in the streets, never to be seen again.

We prayed for another miracle, and we received hundreds of seen and unseen miracles.

The most challenging part of this journey with our son has been battling sadness and grief. We were losing the hopes and dreams we once had for him and living with the devastating reality he may never be able to realize them. We were angry with God for a time and frustrated by His seeming lack of response.

We have come to accept that God was always involved with our son's story, and the Lord never once wavered. He never wanted to see our family go through this awful chapter. But now, in many ways, we have come to understand how the thorns of our son's illness have shaped our hearts and made us more deeply compassionate toward families struggling with similar challenges. We realized we have a choice—we can turn over our anxiety to the Lord or be consumed by fear. Surrendering our angst is the only thing that separates us from those who don't know Jesus.

So many times, even when we were sinners, God was fighting for us before we knew Him. These are the specific ways God has fought for us in the darkness through the valley of the shadow of insanity:

- By opening our eyes to see the truth and by giving us a vision for the future
- By sending angels at just the right time to save us from danger during multiple mental health crises
- By setting a fire in our hearts that is unquenchable until we act
- By saving our son during multiple life-threatening situations
- By allowing us to see this difficult journey from His 30,000-foot perspective, we trust His purposes are more significant than ours

2024

We are happy to say we recently passed the seventh anniversary of the last life-threatening relapse. Our son is amazingly resilient. He now lives and works independently. He manages his medication and therapy. He is drug- and alcohol-free. He has found his passion for auto mechanics by attending night classes at our local community college. He is our hero and our friend.

Some of the best advice we received was from the lead therapist at CooperRiis, a healing community where our son spent six months of his life recovering. She said, "It's important not to 'over-identify' with the illness. Here, clients choose their role in our community. They are the carpenter, the gardener, part of the cleaning crew, or one of the valuable members of our kitchen staff. When they don't show up, it matters to the community."

We are thrilled to watch as our independent, kind, sensitive, and talented 32-year-old son finds traction in his life. Like Rip Van Winkle, sleeping for 20 years, our son is awakening to find his voice and is experiencing life's failures and successes. He is exploring his likes and dislikes and learning to build friendships and relationships. Our son knows he is a part of our family and has our support. He is a business partner and brother; he is an uncle and friend. Most importantly, he is a valuable child of God with a specific purpose only he can fulfill. Yes, managing this mental health challenge for the rest of his life is something he deals with daily, but it does not define him.

We know the road ahead is still uncertain and without guarantees, but we continue to trust God with this journey. Knowing He will be glorified through it all compels us to trust His faithfully provided path.

CHAPTER 19:

Break the Spell

STEVEN VINCENT PHILLIPs was a very strong young man, both in mind and body. When Steven had something on his mind, he didn't hesitate to share, even if it made you feel uncomfortable. He was honest, loving, and generous, especially with his time. He'd do anything for his loved ones and showed up when someone was in need, no matter the inconvenience. When he gave, he gave freely. He was sensitive; he felt things deeply and fully. He was artistic and loved music, channeling his emotions into playing the violin as a child, and later, the piano. Steven also served in the military right out of high school. He loved his family and was fiercely protective of the women in his life. He also had a passion for video games. One day he wanted me to game with him, and I told him I'm not a gamer. "Mom, we're all gamers," he told me. "You're just playing a different game."

After Steven graduated from high school in 2015, he joined the Marine Corps, following in his older brother's footsteps. He graduated from boot camp, and two years later, married the love of his life. He and his wife moved back home to California in 2020 when he was 22, and he enrolled in college using his GI Bill benefits.

Steven had a back injury from his time in the military and began self-medicating with cannabis, which is easily accessible and socially acceptable in California. His wife was initially supportive of his smoking, as it seemed to help with his back pain. When the COVID outbreak began, Steven stopped going to college because everything was shut down. He became isolated and went down a rabbit hole with gaming and weed consumption. He was using high-potency THC pens and dabs. He was high almost all the time. He began experiencing negative effects from the constant use, including an upset stomach, vomiting, and a lack of motivation. He started struggling with paranoid thoughts, sometimes even thinking his wife and his friends were setting him up in some way or another.

Steven's personality changed and became unstable due to his addiction. When he wasn't high, he was agitated; when he was high, he could be lethargic, volatile, or paranoid. This strained his marriage. Steven and his wife went to therapy and began working on a schedule of days he would be allowed to smoke. This helped for a time, but soon his wife found him smoking on days they didn't agree to. He started taking "tolerance breaks," where he would stop smoking for a week or so, and they noticed a huge improvement. He would be less agitated, his stomach issues would subside, and he could keep a more regular sleep schedule. He recognized this and would often say maybe he should tone it back, but he was never able to. After his tolerance breaks, he would return to daily use and his symptoms would return.

His wife didn't know how to help him; she didn't realize he was struggling with addiction because weed is typically thought of as nonaddictive. His mood swings were extreme, and his eyes were sometimes vacant, as if he were unreachable. She felt unsafe around him when he was high, and so she left him. She shared, in hindsight, there were signs early on of how severely Steven's smoking was affecting him, and she wishes she had known more about THC addiction and cannabis-induced psychosis at the time.

In August 2022, Steven came to live with me. It had been over a year since he started smoking heavily, and his addiction was obvious; some mornings he would have an upset stomach and throw up before he had his first smoke. He had a poor appetite and was losing weight. He was depressed and angry with himself. He knew his marijuana use was a major factor in his marriage ending, and he wanted to stop, but couldn't. He would vacillate between recognizing he had a problem and having a "who cares" mentality. He liked the escape and being able to check out and numb himself.

I could see the effects the marijuana was having on his physical and mental health but didn't know what to do or how to help him. I wanted him to know he was loved and valued in his family. I wanted to give him the space and support he needed to figure out the next step in his life.

I tried to encourage Steven to stop using it, and he would occasionally try tolerance breaks. In a journal entry titled "Weed," he wrote that before he smoked, he felt upset about having nothing to do all day but sleep and wake up and wait for low-energy input from a friend. He also added he introspected about "what [he'd] sacrificed at the altar of this substance" and confessed he felt "a little paranoid" in another thought. Steven was aware of the effect THC was having on his mood and mental clarity, but he kept these feelings inside and didn't share. I also didn't realize he was fighting a lot more with withdrawal symptoms than he let on.

Steven wanted something to look forward to and decided to plan a three-month trip to visit his brother, who was stationed in Japan. He bought his tickets and started learning Japanese with a passion, which gave him something positive and tangible to focus on. It felt like a new beginning—a new adventure in his life. He knew marijuana was illegal in Japan and there would be no way of getting it there, so he decided to quit.

He began seriously working on weaning himself off marijuana. He went to visit a friend from the military for a month in Kansas, and during that time he continued to reduce his smoking. He started working out again and attending church services with his friend. When Steven got back home, he was in the best spirits I'd seen him in for months. He wanted to cook and work out together; it was like he had a new lease on life. He used marijuana at night, but overall, his consumption was less, and he had clearly improved significantly.

On April 7, 2023, a few weeks after returning from Kansas, Steven went on a camping trip in the Kern River Canyon with his longtime friend Turner. Though I didn't know it at the time, he took his handgun with him for protection. He was comfortable using firearms and was an advocate for their use as protection. He said goodbye to me for the last time that day. It was still cold, so I gave him his winter coat and told him I loved him. I went to sleep that night not realizing Steven would be in a mental battle for his life just a few hours later.

His friend Turner was a videographer for downhill skaters. About 20 skaters went on the camping trip, but Turner was the only person in the group Steven knew. When Steven arrived at the campsite, it was dark, so Turner helped Steven set up his tent. They joined the others at the bonfire, and Steven socialized and appeared to be having a good time. Steven told Turner about his upcoming trip to Japan and his desire to pursue outreach ministry service when he got back. Turner thought he seemed at peace with where he was in life and excited about his future.

Steven had brought along his THC vape pen and used it that night. Turner also offered Steven a hit off his bong, so Steven and Turner smoked together. Turner reported that in a matter of minutes after taking a hit from the bong, Steven changed completely. He became withdrawn and started shivering and speaking incoherently. Turner thought Steven was joking and tried to laugh it off.

Steven said he was going to bed, and Turner checked on him about 10 minutes later and found he wasn't in his tent and his car was gone. Steven left me a voicemail at 11:50 p.m. while I was sleeping. The message said, "Hey Mom, I'm running out of gas, and I need your help. I'm kind of just sitting somewhere. I drove somewhere, I don't know. I smoked some weed and got stupid, and I need some help. I love you."

Around this same time, Turner called Steven; he answered and said he thought people were trying to kill him, and he was scared and wanted to go home. Turner and another friend drove around trying to figure out Steven's location so they could help him, and Turner instructed Steven to put his hazard lights on. Steven had gotten lost on a dirt road and was bottomed out on a big boulder. During this sequence of events, Steven sent me another text. It read, "Mom please come get me, I'm scared," with coordinates. Then Steven went silent and stopped answering Turner's calls. Steven was alone in his car, scared and paranoid. By the time Turner found him, it was too late.

Steven took his life with his handgun. He made attempts to reach out to his friends and family, but no one was there to help in his moment of panic. My son's death was not planned. He was excited for the future, and he loved his family.

Steven's toxicology report showed THC was the only substance in his system.

I want to honor my son's life by sharing his story in hopes it might help others who are struggling with THC use the way Steven did. I had never heard of cannabis-induced psychosis before this happened to Steven. I want to tell his story so readers will know cannabis-induced psychosis is a real and dangerous thing.

Steven was wise beyond his years. In his short life of 25 years, he taught me what is important and everlasting: listening and being available for others. He would include everyone in a group and never exclude them. He had a love for children and would show them they're just as important as adults. He often would say, "We are all just trying our best." Steven was a gracious young man. He touched the lives of many. Steven will live on in me and all who knew and loved him. I believe he would want to help others from falling into the destructiveness of this drug. I will end in Steven's words:

"I love you, Carry on."

CHAPTER 20:
Marijuana Killed My Soul

I BELONG TO A CLUB no one wants to join. My son Andy died by suicide in March 2014 at the age of 31 in Arizona.

Andy was an Army veteran, a paratrooper with the 82nd Airborne Division. He was a hardworking college graduate. He was a beloved son, brother, nephew, cousin, grandson, and friend to many.

But Andy was tortured by his diagnosed, severe cannabis use disorder.

I have since met other mothers who are also enduring this life change, living with the loss of a child who died young, and trying to heal. I find we mothers feel and behave like all mothers—trying desperately to protect our young. We protect the children we still have, as well as others who are threatened by the same harm that took our own children. Some of us behave like badgers—we are serious and a force to be reckoned with. Like disturbing a bee's nest, we go to work to rebuild our lives while honoring our children who left us far too young.

My son Andy left a suicide note that included these words: "Marijuana killed my soul + ruined my brain."

My son desperately tried to break his marijuana addiction all the way up until his last days. Whenever I hear and read the words that insinuate marijuana has never killed anyone, is harmless, or is not addictive, my heart hurts.

My new friends in "The Club No One Wants to Join" and I work to educate others, especially other young people, and the medical profession. There is a strong relationship between marijuana use, psychosis, and suicide. We want to educate others to prevent further harm, but a terrible thing can happen when we speak out. When we publish our stories, offered in the hope of protecting and educating others, the comments that ensue on social media can be brutal.

We have been called liars. I have been named #FailedParent. I have been told I killed my son. Social media commenters diagnose our children, usually with PTSD and mental illness, and claim marijuana should not be blamed. Since my son was a veteran who served for a few months in Iraq in 2003, I have been told George Bush killed my son.

I have volunteered with an Arizona organization that educates young people about substance abuse. My organization has been criticized for taking advantage of me and my son and told it should be ashamed of its actions.

Who attacks well-meaning parents and community service organizations working for public health? I am never approached personally, thank goodness. Attackers make it clear they support normalizing and commercializing drugs, claiming that approach will be safer for our children. I cannot understand their views, especially now that I look at things from the perspective of a mother missing her wonderful son, who should still be here today.

I am gratified to find, in recent years, there are more parents willing to share their testimonies about the risks and harms of marijuana. There is also more scientific research that confirms our experiences. But I am saddened the media and legislators still pardon and do not acknowledge the drug for the damage done to our families.

I am grateful to organizations like Johnny's Ambassadors that bring light to the issues and problems of THC products and marijuana use and abuse. I am just so sorry my son Andy and Johnny Stack now know each other in an afterlife rather than in life with us here on earth. My Andy would have really enjoyed getting to know Johnny. We miss our children every minute of every day.

I work now to help Andy help others by sharing his warning and working with other families who have been harmed. I have this message for the THC industry:

Dear Marijuana (Cannabis/THC) Industry,

We will no longer fall victim to your scam.

- You said your "miracle drug" would treat and cure a laundry list of illnesses.
- You claimed your drug to be a harmless substance used safely since the dawn of civilization.
- You said, "It's unfair!" that alcohol is a legal drug and marijuana isn't.
- You said, "Kids will be asked for ID at stores to prevent youth use of the drug."
- You promised that drug cartels and the black market would be put out of business by your competition.
- You said racial inequality in drug arrests would be solved.
- You said buckets of taxes would be collected to be directed toward education budgets.
- You said law enforcement was to be freed from work regulating the use of marijuana.

What we now know:

- You took your "natural herb" and modified it into strains of highly potent psychotropic chemicals, increased its power of addiction, and developed enticing new delivery methods.
- Your drug causes an illness called hyperemesis syndrome, or cyclic vomiting.
- Your drug causes cannabis use disorder and creates depression and anxiety.
- Your drug causes psychosis, schizophrenia, and cannabis-induced suicide.
- You market your drug to young people to attract lifelong users.
- You do not ID our kids at your stores. They go to the gray and illegal markets and get it at school and home.
- You located your drug stores in low-income neighborhoods, ensuring the most vulnerable people would become addicted. Drug arrests of people of color have increased, not decreased.
- Your drug increased the illegal market for drugs.
- You set the stage for drug cartels to thrive in legal states such as Colorado, Oregon, Washington, and California. Foreign and domestic cartels have increased the need for local, state, and federal law enforcement.
- You lobby for lower taxes, reducing any potential funding for education.
- Your buckets of taxes? They look like substantial amounts of money, but they are a tiny sliver of a percent in a state budget. Do youth drug use prevention organizations receive any of the taxes collected from the "legal" sales of your drug? Not that we have seen. Instead, we increasingly find schools reluctant to include *your* drug, marijuana, in any drug use prevention education work they do allow.

We will not be complicit in your scam. We will do our best to expose your duplicity.

Sincerely,

- Parents of children who have died because of your drug
- Families of those whose brains and lives have been ruined from use of your drug
- Partners of users who have lost their relationships when your drug became the new love of their life
- Children of parents who neglect or abuse them due to use of your drug
- Employers who cannot find an adequate workforce because they can't pass a drug test from your drug
- Educators who are trying to instruct impaired students, thanks to your drug's odorless delivery systems
- Law enforcement officers are increasingly engaged in regulating the dangerous "legal" market of your drug
- Drug use prevention organizations that are struggling to protect youth from the brain damage caused by your drug

CHAPTER 21:

Threads of Hope

ON JULY 19, 2020, I walked into a store and purchased a journal and daily meditation book. I was desperate to strengthen my faith and process the four-year journey I had been on with my then 22-year-old, THC-addicted son. It was the beginning of a whole new chapter, which still included heartache and hope.

My son was born a beautiful blue-eyed, dark-haired, energetic little boy who had the biggest heart! He was always funny and would do anything for his big sister to include him. In high school, he underwent a subtle transformation, becoming the observant, quiet kid who had a lot of friends and played sports. Freshman year, his dad and I divorced after five years of turmoil that, unfortunately, my kids had to witness. My son seemed to handle things well, continuing to play sports and hang out with friends, while dividing his time between two houses. Little did I know, beneath the surface a struggle was brewing.

My son started smoking weed in high school, unbeknownst to me until his senior year. Despite our conversations, he assured me it was a harmless choice compared to the pitfalls of excessive alcohol consumption. I thought to myself, *It's just weed.* He graduated in 2016 and went to college the following fall.

As a freshman in college, he started dabbing. Somehow, he was able to complete schoolwork, limiting his smoking to nights and weekends. I began paying a little more attention to his actions when a friend of his, who was selling weed, ended up being shot and killed. I was shocked, confused, and scared. I told myself things that kept me in denial and asked my son to distance himself from those who sold weed. He promised me he wasn't involved.

By his second semester of sophomore year, he was smoking or dabbing all day, every day. He ended up failing a class but made it through the year, promising to do better. In his third year of college, he came home one day deeply depressed and anxious, admitting he never got out of bed all day. He was asking for help and told me about another friend who got shot outside his campus apartment for selling weed. This time his friend lived. I responded calmly; however, inside I was questioning how my son, rooted in good values, found himself entangled in this web. How did my child become associated with a world of drugs and danger? No one believed this was happening just over weed.

Opting for a semester off, he moved home and began taking medication for anxiety. The following semester, he was feeling better, so he went back to school. He moved in with different friends who we thought would be a better influence; however, he ended up flunking out. Frustrated and concerned, we decided he needed a break from school, so he moved back home and worked full-time. The panic attacks didn't stop, and he spent days in bed getting high, losing all motivation. He no longer brought friends around, and his relationship with family was becoming nonexistent.

In July 2020, I was introduced to a mom who lost her son to suicide due to psychosis caused by THC. This really opened my eyes, and I started to research, which led me to read Laura Stack's book and join Johnny's Ambassadors. Armed with newfound knowledge, I confronted my son about the damaging effects of THC on the underdeveloped brain and how it can cause psychosis, but he remained unconvinced.

Later that month, my son came home from having lunch with a friend from high school and told me this friend was recovering from being shot on campus for selling weed. A THIRD FRIEND! I felt very alone and desperate, so I decided to try to trust that God would guide me and have my back in getting my son healthy again.

In August 2020, I consulted my childhood best friend, who is a psychologist, and she agreed to talk to my son to try to help. It was the first time the word "addiction" was mentioned. She believed he was using THC to mask feelings he never dealt with related to my divorce, and his bad breakup. She suggested inpatient treatment.

I started researching inpatient programs and quickly realized insurance doesn't cover residential for "just weed" addictions. I was devastated and lost as to what to do. I engaged with my son's dad, and he agreed to come over and join in an intervention. We approached our son about his use and proposed inpatient care. He responded by breaking down and begging us to let him try to quit on his own. We agreed, so we set up some therapy and regular calls with my friend, the psychologist. I also introduced him to Marijuana Anonymous, and he joined a couple of virtual sessions. Faith became my anchor. *Lord, I refuse to sit and do nothing. I choose to get up and step out in faith, trusting you to perform miracles ahead of me.*

In September, after many attempts to quit, my son got angry with me, saying quitting weed would not solve all his problems. He said smoking was the only thing holding him together. He then became emotional and started saying he was nothing but a disappointment in life. He had been gambling and smoking, which led to him quitting his job and spending most of his days in his room sleeping or playing video games. My heart was broken, and I continued to be lost. *God, help me know. Help me know what to do.*

On September 18, 2020, my son and I took off for Lake Powell in Arizona. My friend thought it would be a good reset and advised me to let my son smoke or take Valium as needed to get through the anxiety. It was an amazing trip and helped us grow even closer. When we returned, he decided to try to quit weed again. He got some sober time under his belt, wanted to find a new job, and convinced me smoking weed would help his anxiety so he could work. That following month, he got his medical marijuana card, and I justified it by thinking it was better knowing the weed was clean coming from a dispensary. He continued to apply for jobs, get interviews, and cancel the interviews due to anxiety and panic attacks. By December, his gambling and smoking had gotten worse. He was borrowing money to pay gambling debts and having regular breakdowns over it. He finally agreed to go to Gamblers Anonymous but didn't stick with that program.

In February 2021, we took a trip to Denver to visit his sister and go skiing. While we were there, he got an offer for a job he would start upon his return. We were all very happy for him, and he seemed excited. We had a lot of fun, but I saw firsthand how high his tolerance for weed and Valium was, and upon our return, I noticed he had taken 30 Valium pills while we were there. I freaked out and told him I would hold the Valium and give him one only if he absolutely needed it. I entered a new level of worry and knew in my soul it was time to take more drastic measures to help him.

The new job lasted only a couple of weeks before he resigned due to his constant state of panic. I was so desperate seeing my son slip away that I finally got him help at an outpatient rehab center. In April 2021, he was 10 days sober for the first time since he started smoking in 2015. I saw the light coming back in his eyes, and he finally admitted weed wasn't helping his anxiety but making it worse, and he needed to get clean.

On Mother's Day in 2021, he got 30-plus days sober and started a new job in a warehouse loading and unloading trucks. *Thank You, God, for giving us patience and a little peace!* I thought. *I pray we continue to walk down this path of recovery and that You continue to show us the way.*

On August 6, 2021, I was riding a high! I seemed to have my son back! I was praising God and starting to live again, but by August 23, I was back in hell. My son admitted he lost all the money he made at his job to gambling and was still smoking. The levels of THC in his system went from 80 to 900 ng/mL.

In December 2021, he promised to quit smoking over the holiday and lied to me, saying he was on track. He admitted he needed inpatient care because he couldn't stop smoking and his anxiety was debilitating. I once again did extensive research for inpatient care, but no one would take him if he was only addicted to weed. I became very angry and hopeless, until God created a miracle. My aunt called and informed me she worked at a treatment center in Arizona, and they would get him on a plane the next day. To this day, I call my aunt my angel. My son managed his anxiety and made it to Arizona in January 2022, where he stayed for 40 days. I thought I had my son back. He got great care and therapy and made friends, and then it was time to graduate. We advised him to move to sober living, but he wanted to come home first to see how he would do. He went to a couple of meetings and stayed in touch with the people he met for a few weeks. That all ended, and he felt good enough to move out of my house and live with friends. He landed a job doing quality control for a bank. It was perfect for him, and he loved what he was doing and learning. I really thought this job would help him stay sober, but it didn't.

In September 2023, my son moved back home. He wanted to try to quit again and felt he needed to get away from his living situation to do it. We got him into an outpatient program that would allow him to still work. He seemed to really like the counselors and was doing better, but for the next few months, he would quit, resume using weed, lie about it, feel bad, admit he lied, and call off work due to debilitating anxiety. He decided to take a three-week family medical leave over Christmas to detox with the hope he could return to work anxiety-free once he was weed-free. I *thought* he was doing well—until he wasn't. After I smelled weed in the house, he admitted he never quit. He had lied to me and to the program he was in. He called me from his car in a parking lot breaking down and saying he wanted to drive away and never come home. My heart again was broken as I felt gaslighted and yet empathetic. I knew it was not him—it was the addiction. Where was God???? I was angry. My son is such an amazing kid with the biggest loving heart. Why him? I was humbled and vulnerable realizing I had no power over this. I could only love him and pray. Life is so hard.

On Friday, January 5, 2024, it was a new *Day One*. I dropped my son off at a residential program in our hometown. The only reason insurance covered it was because we entered him into the "mental health" side of the program. It was a 30-day program that would provide group and individual therapy and would cover both the addiction and mental health sides. He seemed fine at drop-off, but after only five hours, I got a call from the center reporting he left against medical advice, and they would have to notify the police. Soon after, my son called me from a gas station pleading for me to pick him up.

He was at a new level of panic, and I felt I had no choice but to bring him home. He claimed it was rock bottom for him. The mental health side of the program was a locked facility for those who might hurt themselves or others, and the place just freaked him out. For the first time, my son saw how his addiction struggles were affecting me, the most important person in his life, he said. I finally broke, and he saw the pure sadness and desperation within me. This triggered him in a positive way. He begged for one more chance to quit via outpatient, so after two days of pure despair, we landed on a partial hospitalization (PHP) program at the same center but a different location. At 25 years old, he is currently 50 days sober. He signed a release so his drug tests will be sent home to me. If his levels don't continue to go down, he will be kicked out of the program and has agreed to then go back to inpatient. These last two weeks have unfolded as a journey of self-discovery, tears, and emotional healing. Each day brings gratitude for sobriety, clarity in my son's eyes, improved appetite due to less anxiety, and a step closer to the life he deserves.

As we navigate this challenging path, I recognize the mistakes made but hope that by sharing our story, we can shed light on the severity of THC addiction. It took years, but he finally realizes THC's potency and its potential to cause harm, which underscores the urgency of raising awareness.

I offer a message of solidarity to those facing similar struggles. You are not alone. Despite the challenges, grace prevails, and there is hope even in the beginning stages of sobriety. Together, we press on, one day at a time, toward healing and a brighter future.

CHAPTER 22

The Sound That Changed My Life Forever

I WILL NEVER FORGET THE SOUND that changed my life forever. It is a sound that is never far from my recollection no matter how much I'd rather forget it. As I sit here reflecting on my life and experiences to share, I struggle already not to cry. I wonder how my hopes and dreams for my child went so wrong. I wish I weren't sharing this with you right now because I wish with all my heart this were not my story, and more importantly, not my oldest son's story. I live in a nightmare I will never wake from, but it didn't start that way.

It started—as many stories do—with a love story. My husband and I dated for five years before marrying, and three years later we had our first son, Nathaniel. I was so happy to be a mother, and my two boys were always the center of my life. Everything I did was in hopes of helping them become happy and fulfilled adults. I encouraged them to develop their interests. Nathaniel from a young age was interested in creating things out of paper, blocks, and anything else he could think of. It started with origami creations that were quite complicated for a 5-year-old. It developed further into creating tanks and ships with minute details that were sometimes only a couple of inches long. People would see them and couldn't believe they were made from paper. He loved to build complex K'nex sets at an age far younger than the recommended age. Even as adults, we shared the love of building LEGO sets. I still have many of his sets, including the Titanic, on display along with my own.

Nathaniel was kind and helped others when he saw the opportunity. People were often surprised when he would open the door for them or help in some other way. He was reliable. If he said he would be somewhere, he would be. He was always on time for work and rarely called in sick, which is why I first became concerned about him that terrible week.

The suddenness of it all still shocks me. At the beginning of that terrible week, I had my normal caring and reliable son. By the end of the week, he was gone. It was like someone flipped a switch and he changed. It was little things at first that we found strange and out of character but dismissed after he would say he was fine. Those things added up that week, but I could never have imagined what they had added up to.

It started on Monday when he didn't go to work. It was very unusual for him to stay home, and I hadn't seen any sign over the weekend he was sick. I asked him why he didn't go to work, and he said he didn't sleep much and didn't feel well. It didn't concern me much at the time, but looking back, it was just the start of many signs.

Tuesday morning came, and he again called in sick for work. Several packages came for him that day, including large containers of military-style, ready-to-eat meals. He was also acting a bit more withdrawn, but that was easier to explain because it was normal for him to spend hours in his room completing a paper model or other project. Those things combined did give me the feeling that something was not quite right, so I knocked on his door to speak with him. He started pacing back and forth when I asked him what was wrong. I had to practically beg him to tell me. After mumbling three times, and me having to ask him to repeat it, he answered, "China is going to kill us all." This was the first time I had heard him state any concern over global political conflicts, so it seemed an odd statement for him. We sat on his bed, and I explained the conflicts and fears people had with other countries in the past, and how those fears were not realized. He seemed to be taking the information in and nodded in agreement. We ended the conversation with a hug that was longer and tighter than I ever recall having in the past. I stood on my tiptoes and kissed him on the cheek and told him I loved him. Looking back, I wonder if the intensity of that hug was a sign I missed.

The next day he got up in the morning and got ready for work like he had every weekday morning before that week. I remember feeling relief that maybe things were returning to normal. I couldn't have been more wrong. He returned from work a little early, but that happened from time to time, depending on the jobs they had for installing the seamless gutters. Later in the day my husband came home and asked if Nathaniel was home. I responded, with a bit of a puzzled "Yes," thinking it should be obvious if he were home with his truck in the driveway. That puzzle was soon solved when my husband asked where his truck was. I had no idea it wasn't there. It was the first time Nathaniel had come home without his truck. When we asked him about it, he made a comment that his boss dropped him off since they were in the area. He acted like he couldn't care less about when he picked it up, which was unusual because that truck had always been important to him. He ordered it brand new and was proud of it. Again, we thought this was odd behavior for him, but we just didn't know what could be going on. He continued to reassure us everything was okay.

We later found out from his boss he had gone to the yard and started packing up like he was quitting. Nathaniel's coworker had called his boss and told him what was going on, so he headed up to the yard to speak with Nathaniel. When he got there, Nathaniel was vaping behind his truck. He sat in his truck with him for quite a while, talking. He stated Nathaniel was telling him how the world was going to end that coming Monday and talked extensively about the conflict with China and the end of the world. His boss was concerned enough that he called the police for a welfare check, and they came to the yard that morning. I don't know much about the details of that visit, but it was resolved with no further action from the police. I knew nothing about it until it was too late. It turns out the real reason he came home without his truck was because he was vaping Delta-8, and his boss had told him he could not drive, or the police would pull him over. The statement I remember most from his boss that day was "He just wasn't Nathaniel." That impacted me because that is exactly how I had felt that week.

Nathaniel did not go to work the rest of the week. He told us he took vacation days for the last two days. Earlier that week, he had stated he would be taking vacation that next week to go camping and to go visit my sister in Ohio, so I didn't think too much of it. During this time, large numbers of packages kept arriving daily. We later found out he had told his coworker he had spent most of his savings of $20,000 on survival supplies. Since he was an adult at 26, we didn't try to get into his business much, so we inquired only a bit about the unusual activity. It was often hard to straddle that line of him being an adult but living with us and being somewhat dependent on us. He was always so responsible before that week, so honestly, there was no need for much concern before then.

On Saturday, August 13, 2022, our world came crashing down on us and we experienced every parent's worst nightmare. The day began normally as we were gradually packing to move closer to family. Nathaniel indicated he was excited about the move and was looking forward to spending time with his younger cousins. I remember sitting on the couch with him as we looked at some of the houses on my tablet that the realtor had sent over. He was actively engaged, telling me what he liked and didn't like. Later, I was packing up in our guest bedroom, which was across from Nathaniel's room and bathroom. I remember thinking it was odd he had gone into the bathroom and had been in there for over an hour, and how it was even stranger that the bathroom light was off much of that time since it was on an automatic sensor. I couldn't shake the gut feeling something was terribly wrong, but I just didn't know what or how to approach him about it outside of continuing to ask him if everything was okay.

Lunchtime approached, and we decided to go to our favorite pizza spot. I called for Nathaniel, and he came out of the bathroom showered and seemingly fine. We had our normal conversations during that lunch. He and my husband made plans to go mountain biking the next day. This was an activity they both enjoyed doing together. Later that day, my husband and I went grocery shopping and brought home rotisserie chicken for dinner. At the dinner table, Nathaniel was unusually quiet and playing with his phone a lot, which was not something he usually did. At one point I could hear my phone messenger pinging in the next room, but I waited to see what those messages were. I finished my dinner first and went to sit on the sofa, which was in the next room of an open-plan living space, so I could still see my son and husband at the table. My husband got up from the table and went into our master bedroom. Meanwhile, I looked at the messages and was surprised to see they were from Nathaniel. I was puzzled because it was a bunch of gibberish that didn't make any sense. I asked him why he sent me that, and he just shrugged and made an "I don't know" sound. He then got up from the table, without taking care of his plate as he normally would and went to his room.

Shortly after, he came out and had his headphones on. He walked out the front door, and a few minutes later, came back in but did not close the door. I found it odd he didn't close the door but thought maybe he was going back out. After waiting several minutes, it didn't appear that was the case, so I got up and closed and locked the door. On my way back to the living room, I saw Nathaniel going to his bathroom and asked him about it. I just got the same shrug. At this point I was very concerned but just didn't know what to do. Shortly after, my husband came out of the master bedroom, and I showed him the texts and told him about the door. I told him something was terribly wrong, and I was really worried about Nathaniel. He took my phone and started to walk toward Nathaniel's room to talk to him about the texts. When he reached the bathroom, we heard the gunshot that will forever be etched in our memories. My husband tried to open the door but found it locked. He kicked it open. I ran to the room, hoping beyond hope it wasn't what I thought it was.

Tragically, when the door gave way, we saw my son lying on the ground, not moving, and a gun in his hand. I told my husband to call 911 since he had my phone in his hand. He did. The 911 operator told him to move the gun and perform CPR until the emergency responders got there. I kept going back and forth to the front door to watch for them to let them in. That felt like the longest 11 minutes of my life. I remember thinking this couldn't be my reality and praying I would wake up from this awful nightmare. Over the months that followed, that sentiment would become a persistent theme.

The rest of that night is etched in my brain forever: The moment the paramedic shook his head as he looked at us to indicate they could not save Nathaniel; the activity in and out of our house as the police had us sit on the front porch while they taped the yellow crime scene tape across the vehicles and pillars on the front porch; and the questions from the detectives about what had happened that night. It all was so surreal. It was something that happened on TV or to other people—not to our family. I kept hoping I would wake up and find out this was all a bad dream.

The weeks and months after that were a blur as I believe I was still in so much shock. My sister flew in with my other son and my daughter-in-law. I will be forever grateful to her, as she was my rock during this time. They helped us go through Nathaniel's room as we struggled to understand why it happened. We found a vaping pen with a partially used cartridge, and the packaging indicated it had 1,000 mg of THC-O, Delta-8 THC, and Delta-10 THC. My son and daughter-in-law had to tell me what those were because I had never even heard of them and was not familiar with vaping materials. We had no idea Nathaniel had started vaping.

I also found a banking statement that showed the purchase just over a week prior. I started to research the product to find out more about it and was surprised by what I found. That information made me believe it contributed to the change in behavior of my son that week. I quickly set up an appointment with my therapist to start to work through the trauma and grief. I described to him the behavior changes and circumstances that took place that week. He asked if he could see the texts Nathaniel sent to me. He indicated he was very familiar with psychosis and believed Nathaniel was suffering from at least a moderate psychosis and was likely hearing voices. Both he and I believe the vaping products of THC-O, Delta-8 THC, and Delta-10 THC-induced psychosis, as he had no prior signs or episodes of mental health issues. I believe my son would be alive today if he had not chosen to consume it. I will never know why he chose to use those products. I just wish he never had.

As you might imagine, this incident has changed our world and who we are now. The pain never goes away when you lose a child. I tell this story so others may know of the dangers of this product and the signs to look for that indicate psychosis and possible suicide. If telling my story can help just one parent avoid the experience of watching their child being wheeled out by the medical examiner in a body bag, then the tears running down my cheeks as I share our story are worth it.

CHAPTER 23:

Psych 101

IT'S JUST POT. That was my attitude when I learned my teenage son was using marijuana. I certainly wasn't happy about it, but I wasn't alarmed.

My son was an honors student, athlete, and community volunteer throughout high school. Before pot, he had no medical or mental health issues.

The summer after my son's junior year of high school, my older son came to me and reported my younger son had confided in him that he had been experimenting with marijuana. I had tried marijuana a few times in high school, so while I wasn't pleased with this information, I thought of it as more or less a rite of passage. What I didn't know, however, was the "pot" my son was using was not the green plant of my youth—it was commercialized, high-potency THC.

Over the following months, my son's mental health steadily declined— from exhibiting irritability to social withdrawal to strange beliefs and fears. At first, we chalked up the changes to normal teenage stress and moodiness. Little by little, over the course of his senior year of high school, my son started expressing odd beliefs about energy, vibrations, and the matrix. He started wearing a crystal on his forehead to protect his head chakra and carrying other crystals in his pockets. He became rail thin, eating very little and restricting his diet to certain foods. He became increasingly irritable and irrational.

By the time my son returned home from his first semester of college, we knew something was wrong. We pleaded with him and tried all different angles to get him to a therapist or psychiatrist, but he adamantly refused. I googled his symptoms over and over, trying to figure out what might be wrong with him, but we couldn't determine anything more than he was delusional and paranoid. But what could we do? He was no longer a minor and was refusing to see a doctor.

All the while, he was continuing to vape high-potency THC.

Only we didn't know it was high-potency THC. We thought it was "just pot." We didn't make any connection between his drug use and these symptoms we were facing.

Our son got worse and worse. It got to the point where we couldn't go out in public because he was so fearful people were stealing his energy. I shared my concerns with my own therapist, with the head of his college's health services, and even called a few psychiatrists' offices to see if they could help. No one could do anything because he was a legal adult. He had to choose to seek help.

His self-care and behavior spiraled downward until his mental state was so debilitating, he became a danger to himself. He had gone days without eating or bathing, he was wearing multiple layers and a winter hat in the heat of the summer, and he was pacing erratically in and out of the house. Not knowing what to do, I called our local hospital. I explained my son was having some kind of mental breakdown and asked what I should do. The nurse who answered the phone asked me, "Ma'am, do you believe your son is a danger to himself or others?" to which I replied I wasn't sure because he appeared to be in a different reality. The nurse explained my son was experiencing a psychotic episode and said I should call 911 and have him taken to the hospital for evaluation.

This was the first time I had come across the word "psychotic" since Psych 101 in college. At that time, they were words on a page to be memorized for a test. Now I was living it, and I knew it must be one of the worst things a person—and their loved ones—could experience. Psychosis is often associated with hallucinations: things people see, hear, or smell that aren't there. It also involves delusions, such as beliefs of grandeur (that you have special powers) or of persecution (that someone or something is after you). My daughter once described psychosis as "seeing your loved one turn into someone you don't recognize."

I followed the nurse's instructions and called 911. After an hour of several police officers and EMTs trying to coax my son into an ambulance, an officer ultimately had to physically tackle him and restrain him on the gurney. Though I went immediately to the hospital to meet him, I could provide no comfort to my son. He was so agitated, so angry, and so out of touch with reality, there was no reasoning with him. I went home and cried, my heart full of anguish for my son, but also with a measure of relief he might finally get the help he needed.

After four days in the emergency department waiting for a bed to be available, followed by a week in the psychiatric hospital, my son was diagnosed with schizophrenia and released. He had been prescribed an antipsychotic, along with strict orders to avoid THC. By then we had come to understand THC was related to psychosis, but we still did not understand to what extent.

After several weeks of medication changes and a subsequent hospitalization (following a marijuana binge), my son was home and doing relatively well. By then we had learned to keep him away from marijuana through supervision and by restricting his access to money. Finally, he was calm, practicing self-care, and engaging in everyday activities with our family. He could carry on a normal conversation—something we had once taken for granted. He was not consumed by fear.

Then one evening, he went to visit a friend. He was healthy and well enough that we thought he could do so independently. When he returned an hour later, the psychosis had already started to set in. The "friend," someone he knew from high school, had sold him a THC vape pen, which he used before returning home. Right before our eyes, my son entered a deep psychosis, terrified that devils were after his soul.

As the evening dragged on, we tried everything to assuage his fears and get him to sleep. Our last attempt was to suggest he try to sleep in the bathtub. Perhaps the devils would not be able to sense him or hurt him through the thick tub walls. He agreed to try. We made up a bed with blankets and a pillow, and I tucked him in. Exhausted myself, I quickly fell asleep. I awoke again at about 1:30 a.m. Waking up spontaneously in the middle of the night was not typical for me; the only explanation I have is my sixth sense was alerting me something was very wrong. My son was gone.

Feeling sick with worry, I sat on the couch and ate a few saltine crackers. I was at a loss of what I could do. In retrospect, I wish I had called 911 and asked for help to find him. But he had wandered the streets before and always returned. I could never have imagined what was about to unfold.

My husband and I received the call around 3 a.m. A police officer informed us our son was at a nearby emergency department, "in pretty bad shape." We rushed to the hospital, our imaginations running wild about what could have happened and what the prognosis might be. I told my husband to drive faster; in case my son was about to die, I didn't want to miss being with him for his last moments. In the emergency department, after a torturous wait, they finally let us see him. We learned first he would live. Then, the next concerns—did he suffer brain damage? Would he be paralyzed?

They did emergency surgery to save the vision in his right eye. Slowly the scans came back. He had no brain damage. No damage to his spinal cord. One side of his face had been completely crushed and would require a metal plate. His jaw was broken in several places and would be wired shut for the next two months. He had lost teeth that would take two years to fully restore. He also suffered lacerations, abrasions, and a broken foot.

It wasn't until the following day that we learned what had happened. That night my son had left the house, climbed up onto a train bridge, and jumped—attempting to kill himself because he believed that was the only way to save his soul from the devils.

After nearly two weeks in the hospital recovering medically, discussions shifted to what would happen next. The psychiatrist and the attending physician strongly recommended he be transferred to a psychiatric hospital—but told me I could make the final decision. We could send him to inpatient care or take him home to participate in an intensive day program. It was the hardest decision I've made in my life. Over the course of his hospital stay—two weeks in which my husband and I took shifts to stay by his side day and night—we had made some progress with gaining his trust and with helping him come to terms with his illness. For someone with a mental illness, with an addiction, or in our case, both, building trust is one of the most powerful tools for recovery. Sending him to the inpatient hospital meant unraveling the progress we had made. He would view "locking him up" as a huge betrayal, and he would be cut off from the relationships I could see were helping him to heal. Yet bringing him home presented a risk to his life. There was no guarantee he wouldn't attempt suicide again; if he did, I knew I would blame myself.

Ultimately, I chose to bring him home. We put an elaborate plan in place. We hired a home caregiver to sit by his door every night so we could sleep knowing he was safe. We created a sign-up sheet for friends and family, so someone was with him every day to visit and keep him company. The goal was to surround him with love and safety and connection.

As a condition of coming home, my son signed an agreement stating he would abstain completely from any THC products. Despite the drastic consequences of his use, it was not easy for him to stop. (A common misconception is marijuana is not addictive.)

Over the following months, we researched and sought out additional support—therapy, a peer mentor, Marijuana Anonymous, and academic support—so he could take some college courses. One resource that was a game changer for our family was the book *I Am Not Sick, I Don't Need Help!* by Xavier Amador. The communication technique developed by Dr. Amador allowed us to repair and strengthen our relationships with my son, so he could trust us and accept our support.

Little by little, my son's brain healed from the damage of THC. The strange beliefs faded over the course of months. His thinking became clearer. His executive functioning improved.

Today, my son still struggles with executive functioning skills, such as planning, focusing, and managing his time. He still finds it difficult to say no to THC, but with the support of his therapist and the 12-step community, he has been largely successful. When he does have minor relapses with THC, we can tell immediately because he becomes withdrawn and irritable. But in the two and a half years since that tragic night, he has not suffered another psychotic episode.

Through support groups and organizations like Johnny's Ambassadors, I have come to personally know dozens of families with stories *just like ours*—happy, healthy young people whose lives were taken off the rails by "just pot." The fortunate among us are supporting children with lifelong illnesses like schizophrenia and bipolar disorder. Sadly, there are many whose children did not survive.

As my family had to learn the hard way, we are now in a world where pot is no longer "just pot." High-potency marijuana and marijuana products like waxes and oils are devastating people's lives. I share our story in hopes it might prevent other families from suffering as we have.

CHAPTER 24:

Sometimes You Must Come Close to Dying to Save Your Life

MY SON'S JOURNEY with marijuana, his subsequent addiction, and eventually his full-blown psychosis began innocently enough when he started smoking weed during his freshman year in college. He suffered from anxiety. I think he initially started using weed to feel accepted in the fraternity, and he believed getting high eased his anxiety.

Connor was a smart, athletic, kind, and loyal young man. He had great friends, was active in a youth group, played baseball throughout high school, and got into a great college. He went from being an AP Scholar and an Illinois State Scholar to getting horrible grades his freshman year of college, especially his first semester. Looking back, we believe his use of marijuana had a lot to do with his lack of focus on school and maintaining high grades. We thought about pulling him out of school, but his grades improved his second semester, and we let him stay.

We were worried he was smoking too much, and his mental health was a concern. The first indication something was off came two years after he started smoking marijuana, when he told us the universe was sending him signs about a girl he was interested in dating. He also was experiencing paranoia and thought he was being followed. These ideations were all part of some very erratic developing behavior. During this time, there were also some ups and downs in his moods, in his behavior, and in his interaction with others. He was very combative at times and had a couple of incidents where he became confrontational with family members, including shoving his sister. He graduated from college in four years and started a job in his field after graduation.

His first psychotic break, due to vaping high-potency THC, came shortly after he started his new job. His manager called me, concerned when Connor didn't show up to the work site and wasn't answering his phone. Unbeknownst to me, my son was getting high before work each morning. He drove to Chicago, threw his phone onto the highway, left his credit card at a restaurant, and spent the day on the beach vaping high-potency THC. I had a gut feeling we would get a call from the police, and we did. Connor had tried to enter the zoo after closing. The zoo park police officer who found him called us and indicated he was behaving very bizarrely. My husband picked our son up, and they had an argument. Connor walked out of the house with nothing on his back; he just walked away. I filed an endangered individual report with the police, and he was found after three days. He didn't want to come home and stayed at a friend's house for another day. Eventually, he realized he needed to come home and was convinced by his friends to go and get treatment for his anxiety and his usage.

He began an intensive outpatient program (IOP) and was given an injectable antipsychotic medication. They diagnosed him with delusional disorder but didn't necessarily make the connection with his excessive THC use. This treatment and therapy helped him during this time, and he was getting better. However, he didn't stop getting high, and after about five months, he stopped taking his medication. His marijuana use decreased for about 18 months (four years from the onset of him smoking weed). He continued to work, see friends, and work out, and he expressed he knew his smoking was a problem.

He started using heavily again, using the high-potency vape pens that can be up to 99 percent THC. His behavior started becoming even more concerning. He said things like, "Do you think there is a heaven above us? That it is in a different place?" And when I would say, "Yes, I do believe there is a heaven above us," he would say, "No, we are living in heaven here on earth," or things such as "No, what we are living in is not real, it is just our imagination."

A few months later, we were taking a family trip to Armenia. I was reluctant to go as Connor's behavior was becoming erratic, and we told him under no circumstance could he bring any cannabis products or paraphernalia with him. We gave him the choice to stay home, but he made the choice to go. While in Armenia for a week, he was very distant, quiet, nonengaged, and edgy. He even blew up at dinner one night at something his older sister said to him and walked out of the restaurant. He kept saying he didn't know why this was happening to him, meaning his delusions and psychosis. In hindsight, he was in THC withdrawal.

We returned from Armenia, and a day later, my son woke me up. I was really disoriented and groggy from jet lag but instantly knew something was very wrong. He was holding two golf clubs and said his dad wasn't who I thought he was. He said his dad was a bad man. I then got a call from a number I didn't recognize, and my husband told me my son attacked him with a golf club. My husband was using a neighbor's cell phone and was concerned my son might harm me. I told him to call 911 and say it was a mental health crisis.

When the police and ambulance arrived, I was able to see my husband was badly beaten. My son had hit him with the golf club, tackled him to the ground, gouged his eye, and was choking him before a neighbor approached and Connor released him. After not smoking or dabbing for a week while we were in Armenia, the use of high-potency THC caused a full-blown psychotic break. He was hospitalized and transferred to a mental health facility and put on a 72-hour hold. We begged the psychiatrist to keep him, but he was released. When he was released, he was taken to jail and then to court, where he was arraigned for domestic battery. I bonded him out, but he couldn't return home due to an order of protection.

Connor continued to vape high-potency THC, was experiencing psychosis, and was spiraling out of control. We hired someone to conduct an intervention and take him to a 90-day inpatient rehab program in Colorado. That program only lasted eight days, and then he walked out of the facility. He came back to Illinois, where we set him up in an extended-stay location.

During this time, he was communicating only with me and insisted it was my husband who attacked him. He asked me to testify in court that he did not assault my husband. When I told him I wouldn't do it, he left for Michigan and blocked me from contacting him. I could see where he was from his banking transactions, and he was in touch with one friend who updated us. We contacted the local police in Michigan as we were concerned that he was a danger to himself and others. He was smoking nonstop, driving high, and when he did finally contact me, he indicated he wanted to harm himself.

He was gone for two months, homeless and psychotic. We got a call from the police when he apparently tried to cash a fraudulent check. He got involved with some dishonest people while he was staying at a shelter, and he unknowingly (while in psychosis) cashed their fraudulent checks and gave them the money for $50. We still didn't know where he was, and then we got a call from him; he was in jail. We got the $2,000 cash for bond and drove six hours to get him out of jail. He looked horrible, he had lost a lot of weight, and I instantly knew he was in psychosis. He made promises and said he wanted to come home and get sober.

We got two rooms at a hotel, and he asked if he could use the car to grab a burger. When I paused, he said, "Don't you trust me?" and I foolishly gave him the keys to the car. When he wasn't back on time, I panicked. I looked at the app for my car and saw he was heading north, toward the Upper Peninsula of Michigan. He had $10 and little gas. I knew he would run out of gas, and we had no way to get to him. I called the police and told them he was having a mental health crisis, wasn't armed or dangerous, and didn't steal my car. I asked them to stop him and tell him to come back to the hotel. The police were able to track him down and pull him over. As the officer was talking to him, my son spouted some expletives at the officer and drove away. He took multiple officers on a wild, late-night car chase, exceeding 120 miles an hour without his lights on. Once his car ran out of gas, the officers caught up with him and confronted him.

We were told he briefly tussled with them, was threateningly brandishing a chair, and dared them to shoot him. He was tased by one of them but managed to escape and run into the nearby wooded area. He was in this wooded area overnight with police trying to find him using a helicopter and search dogs. He spent the night with no coat. Temperatures were in the 30s. He was found the next morning over 8 miles away from where his car had stalled. He was captured after a brief chase and taken to the hospital.

This night was one of the most difficult nights of my adult life. I didn't know if one of the people I loved more than life itself was alive; there was nothing I could do but just hope and pray he would make it through that sleepless night. We were in communication with the police several times throughout the night. I vividly remember the feeling I had that night that the next call we received from them would be a horrible call of a devastating outcome, but thankfully that call never came. I am convinced my son had a guardian angel with him that night. That is the only way I can explain how he made it through to the next day.

Connor was court ordered to an inpatient behavioral health hospital and ordered to take the prescribed medications. He was hospitalized for 21 days and has been sober since the day he was hospitalized. The subsequent challenge of finding providers and the right medications was difficult. The months following his hospitalization were dominated by the worry of dealing with his withdrawal and depression, the concern of lasting impacts from his legal issues, and questions of whether a full recovery from psychosis was possible.

I am proud of my son, of his journey and his recovery. He has been cannabis-free for almost two and a half years and has been sober from alcohol for six months. He recently started a new job and was able to pass the background check. He exercises almost daily, has repaired relationships, and is in a good place. My family continues to heal and move forward.

CHAPTER 25:

Science Is Real

WHERE TO START? At the beginning or end? It is hard to know whether to begin at the "beginning" or at the "end" of our story. Our story began at 6:50 a.m. on September 26, 1996, when a beautiful boy was born into our family. His birth was celebrated with a joyous ring dance by his three older sisters. "He's a boy! He's a boy!" The truth is, there is no end to our story. The nightmare of losing a child never has an ending. There is no last page. No closing of the book.

Fast-forward to March 30, 2018. The only utterance I could muster was "My boy is dead." Or "expired," according to the police officer who came across the street to inform me of what he had found in our son's car. Our boy, dead by his own doing. Suicide. Also found in the car: a creation of charcoal briquettes, alcohol, and drugs, inspired by people who spend their time on the internet preying on the vulnerable—unchecked, unaccountable, invisible, and deadly. Suddenly, I had been transported into a reality TV show. Police, fire, ambulance, yellow tape. A crime scene.

The journey to this moment began years before. Our son—also a brother, grandson, and nephew— brought light and laughter into our lives.

He was a very intelligent, witty, competitive person who excelled at anything he put his mind to. Through his kindness, sensitivity, and openness about his struggles, he connected with those who were fellow travelers on the path. After he passed, we got letters from unknown people speaking of his small acts of humanity—making sure the "old" man at the adult basketball league was always picked for a team; engaging with the kids at school who were overlooked or marginalized by others. The so-called confident "mayor" of middle school. After his passing, we also came to understand to what depths and lengths he went to fund, feed, and hide his addiction, all while excelling academically and athletically, holding down a part-time job, and getting into a great college.

So, what happened? Around ninth grade, there was a shift. Sisters going off to college, transitioning to high school, family stressors, and unbeknownst to us, the introduction of marijuana. Then, a basketball injury sent him on a path to depression, anxiety, and the use of high-potency THC products.

Like many parents, we did all the educating and supporting we could. Therapy, medication, support, recovery programs. Also like many parents, we had no idea about the types of marijuana products out there. It felt like a race against an unknown force that had already infiltrated the life of our child. No parent can imagine the ways the force creeps into one's home and how it hides in plain sight. No idea, yet, as to the lies, denial, dismissal— even in the therapeutic treatment world—about the impact and damage. For what? The almighty dollar. As you weave your way through this cat-and-mouse game of trying to police, contain, educate yourself, plead for help, plead with your child, you deal with the daily abject fear of the unknown.

This may be an appropriate point in our story to share that I, his mother, am a mental health professional. I am well connected professionally and personally in our area across the domains of service, from prevention to intervention. I used every connection I had. While I was lucky enough to have love and support from colleagues, the difficult truth is our systems for recognizing, acknowledging, and treating high-potency THC addiction simply were not there. I had my son's own psychiatrist, an attending physician at a world-renowned facility, assure me, "Once we figure out the right meds for depression and anxiety, this *will* go away." When I explained my son thought THC *was* the treatment for the depression and anxiety, and in moments of clarity even, he was able to say how out of control he felt, how scary the dark thoughts were, how helpless and unlike his former self he felt, we were met with that look they give you.

Our son was denied access to addiction recovery programs because of mental health issues. At that point, no one had acknowledged that persistent marijuana use greatly increases the likelihood of serious psychotic illness. On the flip side, mental health–focused programs were unable to provide the level of addiction recovery services needed to break the cycle. We were on our own to help our son and to help ourselves. We tried desperately to cobble together a series of supports and treatments. We found ourselves running downstairs in the morning to see if he was in bed. Did he go to that 7 a.m. AA meeting that was part of the agreement? Was he in bed? And yes, after the first two suicide attempts, was he alive?

In the end, we tried a sober living home 10 minutes from our house to try to bridge the gap between accountability and recovery, while maintaining a connection to home through family dinners. At the sober living house, he relapsed, made his plan, covered all his bases, and traded on our need to believe, that he—and by extension we—were on a different path. A new beginning.

The wave of emotions and experiences in the months and years following has been both personal to us and frightening, as it is for so many families, some of whom share their stories in this book. Our stories are so similar, we could write for each other. Fear, shock, horror, despair. No aspect of one's life is left untouched. Not a day, not an event, not a birthday or anniversary. The outrage, the questioning, and for some, the call to action. For every one of these stories, there are thousands more who are unknown. Families who are grieving, confused, shamed, and left helpless. The uncounted victims of the "business" of marijuana.

For a period, there were signs in my town and in others that read in part, "Science is real." A value statement among others. Why are we pretending there isn't science widely available that shows us the imperative of protecting developing brains from THC misuse? Are we going to ignore the data on increased hospitalization rates and higher rates of psychosis? Is the increased suicidal ideation, attempts, and completions due to THC outcomes not real science? Are we going to believe those who tout marijuana as a "treatment" for opioid addiction, despite the facts to the contrary?

If you are reading our stories, please understand we share because we know. We share because we do not want any other individual or family to suffer in silence; to not be encouraged to seek recovery, connection, and hope; and to not have their experience recognized as the nightmare it is.

APPENDIX 1

The Bradford Hill Analysis of Causation Applied to Cannabis Use and the Development of Chronic Psychotic Disorders

Christine L. Miller, PhD, Catherine Antley, MD, and Dean Whitlock (editor) with a review and contributions from Carsten Hjorthøj, PhD, Associate Professor, Copenhagen Research Center for Mental Health, University of Copenhagen

(Intent of the Bradford Hill elements as set forth by van Reekum et al., 2001 for neuropsychiatric applications)

van Reekum R, Streiner DL, Conn DK. "Applying Bradford Hill's criteria for causation to neuropsychiatry: challenges and opportunities." *J Neuropsychiatry Clin Neurosci* 13, no. 3 (Summer 2001): 318-25. https://doi.org/10.1176/jnp.13.3.318. PMID: 11514637. https://pubmed.ncbi.nlm.nih.gov/11514637/.

A draft of this Bradford Hill analysis first appeared on IASIC1.org in June 2021.

Epidemiologist Austin Bradford Hill recognized that no one type of study could fully address the causal relationship between an agent and an outcome in human populations. The analysis he developed to categorize the different types of research necessary to substantiate causation has withstood the test of time.

Although not all key elements he defined can be applied to all types of outcomes, in the case of cannabis causing psychosis, their full application is possible. You will find below what we will term "elements of causation" and the studies that satisfy them. This is intended to be a living document, with edits from leading researchers incorporated as more relevant and up-to-date literature is made available. The sequential versions of the document will be archived for the record.

Updated June 4, 2021

Updated March 4, 2024

1. Strength of the association (The stronger the association, the more likely that it is causal.)

> **Daily use of marijuana with a low to moderate potency of Δ9-tetra-hydrocannabinol (THC) increases the risk of psychotic outcome by 4 to 5-fold, respectively (Marconi et al., 2016; Di Forti et al., 2015), a very strong association. Moderate potency includes what is known as "skunk" in the UK, which, at ~10% to 15% THC, was considered high potency in the UK but moderate potency by US standards.**
>
> **Di Forti M, Marconi A, Carra E, Fraietta S, Trotta A, Bonomo M, Bianconi F, Gardner-Sood P, O'Connor J, Russo M, Stilo SA, Marques TR, Mondelli V, Dazzan P, Pariante C, David AS, Gaughran**

F, Atakan Z, Iyegbe C, Powell J, Morgan C, Lynskey M, Murray RM. "Proportion of patients in south London with first-episode psychosis attributable to use of high potency cannabis: a case-control study." *The Lancet Psychiatry* 2, no. 3 (2015): 233-8. https://www. thelancet.com/journals/lanpsy/article/PIIS2215-0366(14)00117-5/ fulltext.

Marconi A, Di Forti M, Lewis CM, Murray RM, Vassos E. "Meta-analysis of the Association Between the Level of Cannabis Use and Risk of Psychosis." *Schizophr Bull* 42, no.5 (2016): 1262-9. https:// www.ncbi.nlm.nih.gov/pmc/articles/PMC4988731/.

2. Consistency of the evidence (Consistent findings observed by different researchers in different places with different types of subjects strengthens the likelihood of an effect.)

i. **Two large meta-analyses of studies into the association between cannabis use and psychosis have been published, one in 2007 (Moore et al.) and one in 2016 (Marconi et al.), in total covering research from the USA, Germany, the Netherlands, the UK, Sweden, New Zealand, Australia, and Finland.** The types of data ranged from cross-sectional case-control comparisons in catchment areas or registries, to prospective studies and birth cohorts. The subjects varied in age range as well as in occupation, from the general population to military conscripts. The two meta-analyses covered a range of potencies and use frequencies and overlapped in six studies but did not overlap for five. Both reported a significant association between marijuana use and psychosis and/or schizophrenia. Although a few studies have found no significant association, most have either been too small in size to detect, at a minimum, the 1.8-fold increase in risk reported by Moore et al.;

e.g., Bechtold et al., 2015) did not obtain adequate data on use frequency ("ever use" versus more frequent use) and/or analyzed the prior use of marijuana/followed the subjects over too short a period of time, e.g., Phillips et al., 2002).

Bechtold J, Simpson T, White HR, Pardini D. "Chronic Adolescent Marijuana Use as a Risk Factor for Physical and Mental Health Problems in Young Adult Men." *Psychol Addict Behav*. 29, no. 3 (Sep 2015) :552-63. https://doi.org/10.1037/adb0000103. Epub 2015 Aug 3. Erratum in: *Psychol Addict Behav*. 29, no. 4 (Dec 2015): ix-x. PMID: 26237286; PMCID: PMC4586320. https://www.ncbi.nlm.nih.gov/pmc/articles/PMC4586320/pdf/nihms-700940.pdf.

Marconi A, Di Forti M, Lewis CM, Murray RM, Vassos E. "Meta-analysis of the Association Between the Level of Cannabis Use and Risk of Psychosis." *Schizophr Bull*. 42, no. 5 (2016): 1262-9. https://www.ncbi.nlm.nih.gov/pmc/articles/PMC4988731/.

Moore TH, Zammit S, Lingford-Hughes A, Barnes TR, Jones PB, Burke M, Lewis G. "Cannabis use and risk of psychotic or affective mental health outcomes: a systematic review." *The Lancet* 370, no. 9584 (Jul 2007): 319-28. https://doi.org/10.1016/S0140-6736(07)61162-3. PMID: 17662880. https://pubmed.ncbi.nlm.nih.gov/17662880/.

Phillips LJ, Curry C, Yung AR, Yuen HP, Adlard S, McGorry PD. "Cannabis Use Is Not Associated with the Development of Psychosis in an 'Ultra' High-Risk Group." *Aust N Z J Psychiatry* 36, no. 6 (Dec 2002): 800-6. https://doi.org/10.1046/j.1440-1614.2002.01089.x. PMID: 12406123. https://pubmed.ncbi.nlm.nih.gov/12406123/.

ii. **In addition to research results included in the preceding meta-analyses, many relevant publications have occurred since that time. Both small and large research projects worldwide have continued to find a significant association between cannabis use and psychosis/schizophrenia, including but not limited to the following reports**: in 11 different cities in Europe (Di Forti et al., 2019); in a countrywide registry-based study in Denmark (Nielsen et al., 2017), and a Danish population-level study illustrating that as cannabis use disorder (CUD) rates increased, the incidence of schizophrenia increased (Hjorthøj et al., 2021) as well as a more recent countrywide registry-based study by the same first author (Hjorthøj et al., 2023) finding that the population-attributable fraction for CUD in those with schizophrenia peaked at 30% in males aged 21–25; in a prospective study from Finland (Mustonen et al., 2018); in a population-based case-control study from a hospital in Africa (Lasebikan and Aremu, 2018); in a large case-control study from the USA that assessed use frequency (Davis et al., 2013); in a retrospective temporal study of a first-episode psychosis population in the USA (Kelley et al., 2016); in a population-based study from Canada (Maloney-Hall et al., 2020); and in case-control reports from South America (Allende Serra et al., 2019; Libuy et al., 2018).

Alliende Serra LM, Castañeda Agüero CP, Iruretagoyena B, Undurraga J, González A, Crossley N. "T67. Case-control Study of Cannabis Use in First-episode Psychosis in Chile." *Schizophr Bull.* 45, suppl. 2 (2019): S230. https://www.researchgate.net/profile/Juan- Undurraga/publication/332313855_T67_Case_control_study of cannabis use in first_episode_psychosis_in_Cjille/links/5d5b680e92851c37636bd344/T67-case-control-study- of-cannabis-use-in-first-episode-psychosis-in-Chile.pdf.

Davis GP, Compton MT, Wang S, Levin FR, Blanco C. "Association between cannabis use, psychosis, and schizotypal personality disorder: Findings from the National Epidemiologic Survey on Alcohol and Related Conditions." *Schizophr Res.* 151, no. 1–3 (Dec 2013): 197-202. https://doi.org/10.1016/j.schres.2013.10.018. Epub 2013 Nov 5. PMID: 24200416; PMCID: PMC3877688. https://www.ncbi.nlm.nih.gov/pmc/articles/PMC3877688/pdf/nihms534094.pdf.

Di Forti M, Quattrone D, Freeman TP, Tripoli G, Gayer-Anderson C, Quigley H, et al., EU-GEI WP2 Group. "The contribution of cannabis use to variation in the incidence of psychotic disorder across Europe (EU-GEI): a multicentre case-control study." *The Lancet Psychiatry* 6 (March 19, 2019): 427-36. https://www.thelancet.com/action/showPdf?pii=S2215-0366%2819%2930048-3.

Hjorthøj C, Posselt CM, Nordentoft M. "Development Over Time of the Population-Attributable Risk Fraction for Cannabis Use Disorder in Schizophrenia in Denmark." *JAMA Psychiatry* 78, no. 9 (Sep 2021): 1013-19. https://doi.org/10.1001/jamapsychiatry.2021.1471. https://jamanetwork.com/journals/jamapsychiatry/article-abstract/2782160.

Hjorthøj C, Compton W, Starzer M, Nordholm D, Einstein E, Erlangsen A, Nordentoft M, Volkow ND, Han B. "Association between cannabis use disorder and schizophrenia stronger in young males than in females." *Psychological Medicine* 4 (May 2023): 1-7. https://www.cambridge.org/core/services/aop-cambridge-core/content/view/E1F8F0E09C6541CB8529A326C3641A68/S0033291723000880a.pdf/association-between-cannabis-use-disorder-and-schizophrenia-stronger-in-young-males-than-in-females.pdf.

Nielsen SM, Toftdahl NG, Nordentoft M, Hjorthøj C. "Association between alcohol, cannabis, and other illicit substance abuse and risk of developing schizophrenia: a nationwide population-based register study." *Psychol Med.* 47, no. 9 (Jul 2017): 1668-1677. https://doi.org/10.1017/S0033291717000162. Epub 2017 Feb 7. PMID: 28166863. https://pubmed.ncbi.nlm.nih.gov/28166863/.

Kelley ME, Wan CR, Broussard B, Crisafio A, Cristofaro S, Johnson S, Reed TA, Amar P, Kaslow NJ, Walker EF, Compton MT. "Marijuana use in the immediate 5-year premorbid period is associated with increased risk of onset of schizophrenia and related psychotic disorders." *Schizophr Res.* 171, no. 1–3 (Mar 2016): 62-7. https://doi.org/10.1016/j.schres.2016.01.015. Epub 2016 Jan 17. PMID: 26785806; PMCID: PMC4929616. https://www.ncbi.nlm.nih.gov/pmc/articles/PMC4929616/pdf/nihms752585.pdf.

Lasebikan V, Aremu OO. "Cannabis Use and Associated Harms among Schizophrenia Patients in a Nigerian Clinical Setting: A Case-Control Study." *Front Psychiatry* 7 (Aug 2016): 136. https://doi.org/10.3389/fpsyt.2016.00136. PMID: 27536254; PMCID: PMC4971430. https://www.ncbi.nlm.nih.gov/pmc/articles/PMC4971430/pdf/fpsyt-07-00136.pdf.

Libuy N, de Angel V, Ibáñez C, Murray RM, Mundt AP. "The relative prevalence of schizophrenia among cannabis and cocaine users attending addiction services." *Schizophr Res.* 194 (Apr 2018): 13-17. https://doi.org/10.1016/j.schres.2017.04.010. Epub 2017 Apr 18. PMID: 28427930. http://repositorio.uchile.cl/bitstream/handle/2250/149979/The-relative-prevalence-of- schizophrenia.pdf?sequence=1.

Maloney-Hall B, Wallingford SC, Konefal S, Young MM. "Psychotic disorder and cannabis use: Canadian hospitalization trends, 2006–2015." *Health Promot Chronic Dis Prev Can.* 40, no. 5–6 (Jun 2020):

176-183. https://doi.org/10.24095/hpcdp.40.5/6.06. PMID: 32529977; PMCID: PMC7367424. https://www.ncbi.nlm.nih.gov/pmc/articles/ PMC7367424/pdf/40_5-6_6.pdf.

Mustonen A, Niemelä S, Nordström T, Murray GK, Mäki P, Jääskeläinen E, Miettunen J. "Adolescent cannabis use, baseline prodromal symptoms and the risk of psychosis." *Br J Psychiatry* 212, no. 4 (Apr 2018): 227-233. https://doi.org/10.1192/bjp.2017.52. PMID: 29557758. https://pubmed. ncbi.nlm.nih.gov/29557758/.

3. Specificity (This element of causation dates to a time when one agent was considered causative of one outcome, before science had advanced to an understanding of the complexity of outcomes from one agent, and the number of agents that can cause a similar outcome, as described by van Reekum et al., 2001. Although the Specificity element of causation is limited in its application, it can be considered in the cannabis–psychosis connection in two respects: 1) the effect size of cannabis relative to other drugs of abuse and 2) with respect to the population-attributable fraction size for cannabis as compared to that of family history risk.)

i. **How marijuana compares to other recreational drugs in the progression from temporary psychosis to schizophrenia: the effect size of cannabis surpasses all other drugs**—i.e., as compared to other hallucinogens, cocaine, amphetamines, opioids, or alcohol (Niemi-Pynttäri et al., 2013; Starzer et al., 2018). Nearly 50% of cases of cannabis-induced psychosis transition to a chronic psychotic disorder, and the other drugs do so at a lower rate.

Niemi-Pynttäri JA, Sund R, Putkonen H, Vorma H, Wahlbeck K, Pirkola SP. "Substance-Induced Psychoses Converting Into Schizophrenia: A Register-Based Study of 18,478 Finnish Inpatient Cases." *J Clin Psychiatry* 74, no. 1

(2013): e94. https://www.psychiatrist.com/jcp/article/Pages/2013/v74n01/v74n0115.aspx.

Starzer MSK, Nordentoft M, Hjorthøj C. "Rates and Predictors of Conversion to Schizophrenia or Bipolar Disorder Following Substance-Induced Psychosis." *Am J Psychiatry* 175, no. 4 (2018): 343-350. https://ajp.psychiatryonline.org/doi/abs/10.1176/appi.ajp.2017.17020223?rfr_dat=cr_pub%3Dpubmed&url_ver=Z39.88-2003&rfr_id=ori%3Arid%3Acrossref.org&journalCode=ajp

ii. **The fraction of schizophrenia cases attributable (Population Attributable Fraction PAF) to heavy use of higher potency cannabis use exceeds the PAF for family history of psychosis.**

The PAF for first-degree family history in schizophrenia cases is reported to be 5.5%, and the PAF for a first- or second-degree family history in schizophrenia cases is reported to be between 12% (Boydell et al., 2007) and 26% (Ruhrmann et al., 2010). Reaching out to third-degree relatives reduces the effect size such that it is not meaningfully different than the family history of the non-affected population.

The PAF for cannabis use in schizophrenia cases depends on the potency and use rates, ranging from 8% for low potency cannabis (Arseneault et al., 2004) up to 50% for heavy use of higher potency cannabis by a significant proportion of the population (Di Forti et al., 2019).

Arseneault L, Cannon M, Witton J, Murray RM. "Causal association between cannabis and psychosis: examination of the evidence." *Br J Psychiatry* 184 (Feb 2004): 110-17. https://doi.org/10.1192/bjp.184.2.110. PMID: 14754822. https://pubmed.ncbi.nlm.nih.gov/14754822/.

Boydell J, Dean K, Dutta R, Giouroukou E, Fearon P, Murray R. "A comparison of symptoms and family history in schizophrenia with and without prior cannabis use: implications for the concept of cannabis psychosis." *Schizophr Res* 93, no. 1–3 (2007): 203-10. https://www.sciencedirect.com/science/article/pii/S0920996407001508?via%3Dihub.

Di Forti M, Marconi A, Carra E, Fraietta S, Trotta A, Bonomo M, Bianconi F, Gardner-Sood P, O'Connor J, Russo M, Stilo SA, Marques TR, Mondelli V, Dazzan P, Pariante C, David AS, Gaughran F, Atakan Z, Iyegbe C, Powell J, Morgan C, Lynskey M, Murray RM. "Proportion of patients in south London with first-episode psychosis attributable to use of high potency cannabis: a case-control study." *The Lancet Psychiatry* 2, no. 3 (2015): 233-8. https://www.thelancet.com/journals/lanpsy/article/PIIS2215-0366(14)00117-5/fulltext.

Mortensen PB, Pedersen CB, Westergaard T, Wohlfahrt J, Ewald H, Mors O, Andersen PK, Melbye M. "Effects of Family History and Place and Season of Birth on the Risk of Schizophrenia." *N Engl J Med* 340, no. 8 (Feb 25, 1999): 603-8. https://doi.org/10.1056/NEJM199902253400803. PMID: 10029644. https://www.nejm.org/doi/pdf/10.1056/NEJM199902253400803?articleTools=true.

Ruhrmann S, Schultze-Lutter F, Salokangas RK, Heinimaa M, Linszen D, Dingemans P, Birchwood M, Patterson P, Juckel G, Heinz A, Morrison A, Lewis S, von Reventlow HG, Klosterkötter J. "Prediction of Psychosis in Adolescents and Young Adults at High Risk: Results from the Prospective European Prediction of Psychosis Study." *Arch Gen Psychiatry* 67, no. 3 (2010): 241-51. https://jamanetwork.com/journals/jamapsychiatry/fullarticle/210635.

Starzer MSK, Nordentoft M, Hjorthøj C. "Rates and Predictors of Conversion to Schizophrenia or Bipolar Disorder Following Substance-Induced Psychosis." *Am J Psychiatry* 175, no. 4 (2018): 343-350. https://ajp. psychiatryonline.org/doi/abs/10.1176/appi.ajp.2017.17020223?rfr_dat=cr_ pub%3Dpu bmed&url_ver=Z39.88-2003&rfr_id=ori%3Arid%3Acrossref. org&journalCode=ajp.

4. Temporality (The effect must occur after the cause, and in this case, the concept is important to rule out self-medication as a driver of the association.)

In prospective studies, cannabis use has been found to significantly predict developing psychosis (Arseneault et al., 2002; Henquet et al., 2005; Kuepper et al., 2011; Mustonen et al., 2018; van Os et al., 2020), whereas psychotic symptoms at study onset, including those that are prodromal in nature, have generally not been predictive of commencing cannabis use. However, evidence for some degree of bi-directionality exists (psychosis leading to cannabis use) in almost all the prospective studies, and it reached significance in the work of Griffith-Lendering et al., (2013). Incipient, "prodromal" symptoms of psychosis appeared to have significantly increased the propensity to commence cannabis use, as well as vice versa. Yet critics of the Griffith-Lendering study have pointed to the use of questionnaires to collect the prodromal data rather than clinical interviews common in the other research reports, which from our perspective, may have resulted in overly inclusive responses to poorly phrased questions relevant to prodromal symptoms. For example, the question pertaining to "seeing things that other people do not see" could be misinterpreted to mean having insight into things that other people fail to perceive, a misunderstanding that a clinical interview could correct.

Arseneault L, Cannon M, Poulton R, Murray R, Caspi A, Moffitt TE, 2002, "Cannabis use in adolescence and risk for adult psychosis: longitudinal prospective study." *BMJ* 325, no. 7374 (2002): 1212-13. https://www.ncbi. nlm.nih.gov/pmc/articles/PMC135493/pdf/1212.pdf.

Henquet C, Krabbendam L, Spauwen J, et al. "Prospective cohort study of cannabis use, predisposition for psychosis, and psychotic symptoms in young people." *BMJ* 330 (2005): 11–15. http://www.ncbi.nlm.nih.gov/pmc/ articles/PMC539839/pdf/bmj33000011.pdf.

Griffith-Lendering MF, Wigman JT, Prince van Leeuwen A, Huijbregts SC, Huizink AC, Ormel J, Verhulst FC, van Os J, Swaab H, Vollebergh WA. "Cannabis use and vulnerability for psychosis in early adolescence—a TRAILS study." *Addiction* 108, no. 4 (Apr 2013): 733-40. https:// doi.org/10.1111/add.12050. Epub 2013 Jan 3. PMID: 23216690. https:// pubmed.ncbi.nlm.nih.gov/23216690/.

Kuepper R, van Os J, Lieb R, Wittchen HU, Höfler M, Henquet C. "Continued cannabis use and risk of incidence and persistence of psychotic symptoms: 10-year follow-up cohort study." *BMJ* 1, no. 342 (Mar 2011): d738. https://doi.org/10.1136/bmj.d738. https://pubmed.ncbi.nlm.nih. gov/21363868/.

Mustonen A, Niemelä S, Nordström T, Murray GK, Mäki P, Jääskeläinen E, Miettunen J. "Adolescent cannabis use, baseline prodromal symptoms and the risk of psychosis." *Br J Psychiatry* 212, no. 4 (2018): 227-233. https:// www.cambridge.org/core/services/aop-cambridge- core/content/view/ D5CAA12A5F424146DABB9C6A6AB4CB56/S0007125017000526a.pdf/ ad olescent_cannabis_use_baseline_prodromal_symptoms_and_the_risk_ of_psychosis.pdf.

van Os J, Pries LK, Ten Have M, de Graaf R, van Dorsselaer S, Bak M, Wittchen HU, Rutten BPF, Guloksuz S. "Schizophrenia and the Environment: Within-Person Analyses May be Required to Yield Evidence of Unconfounded and Causal Association—The Example of Cannabis and Psychosis." *Schizophr Bull* 47, no. 3 (Apr 29, 2021): 594-603. https://doi.org/10.1093/schbul/sbab019. PMID: 33693921; PMCID: PMC8084443. https://www.ncbi.nlm.nih.gov/pmc/articles/PMC8084443/pdf/sbab019.pdf.

5. Biologic Gradient (Has a dose-response relationship, which in pharmacology is considered to be one important element for illustrating that a drug causes a certain outcome.)

Dose-response correlations demonstrate that the heavier the use of cannabis and the more potent the THC content, the more likely a psychotic outcome.

Andréasson S, Engström A, Allebeck P, Rydberg U. "Cannabis and schizophrenia. A Longitudinal Study of Swedish Conscripts." *The Lancet* 330, no. 8574 (Dec 1987): 1483-1486. https://www.thelancet.com/journals/lancet/article/PIIS0140-6736(87)92620-1/fulltext.

Arseneault L, Cannon M, Poulton R, Murray R, Caspi A, Moffitt TE. "Cannabis use in adolescence and risk for adult psychosis: longitudinal prospective study." *BMJ* 325, no. 7374 (2002): 1212-13. https://www.ncbi.nlm.nih.gov/pmc/articles/PMC135493/pdf/1212.pdf.

Davis GP, Compton MT, Wang S, Levin FR, Blanco C. "Association between cannabis use, psychosis, and schizotypal personality disorder: findings from the National Epidemiologic Survey on Alcohol and Related Conditions." *Schizophr Res* 151, no. 1–3 (2013): 197-202. https://www.ncbi.nlm.nih.gov/pmc/articles/PMC3877688/pdf/nihms534094.pdf.

DiForti M, Morgan C, Dazzan P, Pariante C, Mondelli V, Marques TR, Handley R, Luzi S, Russo M, Paparelli A, Butt A, Stilo SA, Wiffen B, Powell J, Murray RM. "High-potency cannabis and the risk of psychosis." *Br J Psychiatry* 195, no. 6 (2009): 488-91. https://www.ncbi.nlm.nih.gov/pmc/articles/PMC2801827/?report=printable.

Di Forti M, Marconi A, Carra E, Fraietta S, Trotta A, Bonomo M, Bianconi F, Gardner-Sood P, O'Connor J, Russo M, Stilo SA, Marques TR, Mondelli V, Dazzan P, Pariante C, David AS, Gaughran F, Atakan Z, Iyegbe C, Powell J, Morgan C, Lynskey M, Murray RM. "Proportion of patients in south London with first-episode psychosis attributable to use of high potency cannabis: a case-control study." *The Lancet Psychiatry* 2, no. 3 (2015): 233-8 https://www.thelancet.com/journals/lanpsy/article/PIIS2215-0366(14)00117-5/fulltext.

Marconi A, Di Forti M, Lewis CM, Murray RM, Vassos E. "Meta-analysis of the Association Between the Level of Cannabis Use and Risk of Psychosis." *Schizophr Bull.* 42, no. 5 (2016): 1262-9. https://www.ncbi.nlm.nih.gov/pmc/articles/PMC4988731/.

Moore TH, Zammit S, Lingford-Hughes A, Barnes TR, Jones PB, Burke M, Lewis G. "Cannabis use and risk of psychotic or affective mental health outcomes: a systematic review." *The Lancet* 370, no. 9584 (Jul 28, 2007): 319-28. https://doi.org/10.1016/S0140-6736(07)61162-3. PMID: 17662880. https://pubmed.ncbi.nlm.nih.gov/17662880/.

van Os J, Bak M, Hanssen M, Bijl RV, de Graaf R, Verdoux H. "Cannabis use and psychosis: a longitudinal population-based study." *Am J Epidemiol* 156, no. 4 (2002): 319-27. https://www.ncbi.nlm.nih.gov/pubmed/12181101.

Zammit S, Allebeck P, Andréasson S, Lundberg I, Lewis G. "Self-reported cannabis use as a risk factor for schizophrenia in Swedish conscripts of 1969: historical cohort study." *BMJ* 325, no. 7374 (Nov 23, 2002): 1199. http://www.bmj.com/content/325/7374/1199.full.pdf.

6. Plausibility (a plausible biological mechanism) and **7. Coherence** (the coherence between a plausible biological mechanism and what is already known about the disease—see van Reekum et al., 2001, above). These two elements of causation are best discussed together, and it must be noted that the plausible mechanisms are not mutually exclusive, nor do they preclude other more important mechanisms being added to an understanding of the phenomenon as they are uncovered.

i. **A plausible mechanism concerning dopamine and coherence with what is already known about a chronic psychotic disorder like schizophrenia:** Similar to other drugs of abuse, THC has been shown to increase dopamine synthesis and release in the brain in the majority of animal models (reviewed by Bloomfield et al., 2016) and in human studies (Bossong et al., 2015). Much work has been done illustrating over-activity of the catecholamine dopamine in psychotic disorders like schizophrenia, and most antipsychotic drugs block one or more of the dopamine receptors (reviewed by Seeman et al., 2013), though other interactions of the antipsychotic drugs with catecholamine or indoleamine function may also contribute to their mechanism of action (Miller, 2013).

Bloomfield MA, Ashok AH, Volkow ND, Howes OD. "The effects of Δ^9-tetrahydrocannabinol on the dopamine system." *Nature* 539, no. 7629 (Nov 17, 2016): 369-377. https://doi.org/10.1038/nature20153. PMID: 27785201; PMCID: PMC5123717. https://www.ncbi.nlm.nih.gov/pmc/articles/PMC5123717/.

Bossong MG, Mehta MA, van Berckel BN, Howes OD, Kahn RS, Stokes PR. "Further human evidence for striatal dopamine release induced by administration of Δ9-tetrahydrocannabinol (THC): selectivity to limbic striatum." *Psychopharmacology* 232, no. 15 (Aug 2015): 2723-9. https://doi.org/10.1007/s00213-015-3915-0. Epub 2015 Mar 25. PMID: 25801289; PMCID: PMC4816196. https://www.ncbi.nlm.nih.gov/pmc/articles/PMC4816196/pdf/emss-66024.pdf.

Miller CL. "On the mechanism of action of antipsychotic drugs: a chemical reaction not receptor blockade." *Curr Drug Discov Technol.* 10, no. 3 (2013): 195-208. https://pubmed.ncbi.nlm.nih.gov/23363232/.

Seeman P. "Schizophrenia and dopamine receptors." *Eur Neuropsychopharmacol* 23, no. 9 (Sep 2013): 999-1009. https://doi.org/10.1016/j.euroneuro.2013.06.005. Epub 2013 Jul 13. PMID: 23860356. https://pubmed.ncbi.nlm.nih.gov/23860356/.

ii. **A plausible mechanism concerning the kynurenine pathway and coherence with what is already known about schizophrenia and bipolar disorder with psychosis**: THC has been shown to activate the kynurenine pathway in immune cells, in the concentration range known to be intoxicating, from 10 ng/ml up to several hundred ng/ml (Jenny et al., 2009). Although the immune cells themselves should not cross the blood brain barrier, two of the pathway intermediates can (kynurenine and 3-hydroxykynurenine; Schwarcz et al., 2012). In addition, the older literature on animal models demonstrated that THC increased the activity of one of the initiating enzymes of the pathway (tryptophan 2,3–dioxygenase) in the liver (Poddar and Gosh, 1972). This is coherent with what is known about schizophrenia because many studies have shown an upregulation in kynurenine pathway enzymes and metabolites in psychotic disorders, including schizophrenia (Schwarcz et al., 2001; Miller et al., 2006; reviewed more recently by Chiapelli et al., 2018).

Chiappelli J, Notarangelo FM, Pocivavsek A, Thomas MAR, Rowland LM, Schwarcz R, Hong LE. "Influence of plasma cytokines on kynurenine and kynurenic acid in schizophrenia." *Neuropsychopharmacology* 43, no. 8 (Jul 2018): 1675-1680. http://doi.org/10.1038/s41386-018-0038-4. Epub 2018 Feb 27. PMID: 29520060; PMCID: PMC6006321. https://www.ncbi. nlm.nih.gov/pmc/articles/PMC6006321/pdf/41386_2018_Article_38.pdf.

Jenny M, Santer E, Pirich E, Schennach H, Fuchs D. "Δ9-Tetrahydrocannabinol and cannabidiol modulate mitogen-induced tryptophan degradation and neopterin formation in peripheral blood mononuclear cells in vitro." *J Neuroimmunol* 207, no. 1–2 (Feb 15, 2009): 75-82. https://doi.org/10.1016/j.jneuroim.2008.12.004. Epub 2009 Jan 22. PMID: 19167098. https://pubmed.ncbi.nlm.nih.gov/19167098/.

Miller CL, Llenos IC, Dulay JR, Weis S. "Upregulation of the initiating step of the kynurenine pathway in postmortem anterior cingulate cortex from individuals with schizophrenia and bipolar disorder." *Brain Res.* 1073-1074 (Feb 16, 2006): 25-37. https://doi.org/10.1016/j.brainres.2005.12.056. Epub 2006 Jan 30. PMID: 16448631. https://pubmed.ncbi. nlm.nih.gov/16448631/.

Poddar MK, Ghosh JJ. "Effect of cannabis extract, Δ^9-tetrahydrocannabinol and lysergic acid diethylamide on rat liver enzymes. *Biochem Pharmacol.* 21, no. 24 (1972): 3301-3. https://pubmed. ncbi.nlm.nih.gov/4405370/.

Schwarcz R, Bruno JP, Muchowski PJ, Wu HQ. "Kynurenines in the mammalian brain: when physiology meets pathology." *Nat Rev Neurosci.* 13, no. 7 (Jul 2012): 465-77. https://doi.org/10.1038/nrn3257. PMID: 22678511; PMCID: PMC3681811. https://www.ncbi.nlm.nih.gov/pmc/ articles/PMC3681811/pdf/nihms468169.pdf.

Schwarcz R, Rassoulpour A, Wu HQ, Medoff D, Tamminga CA, Roberts RC. "Increased cortical kynurenate content in schizophrenia." *Biol Psychiatry* 50, no. 7 (2001): 521–530. https://pubmed.ncbi.nlm.nih.gov/11600105/.

iii. **A plausible mechanism concerning structural changes to the brain and coherence with what is already known about schizophrenia:** The strongest studies of brain structure are those that are longitudinal in nature, i.e., that follow the same individuals over time. In one such study employing MRI scans, Yu et al. (2020) found developmental differences in the right parahippocampal gyrus (a lowered expansion of the uncus) in cannabis users with psychotic experiences. Coherent with this finding, in a cross-sectional study of early schizophrenia patients, Du et al., 2018) found a reduced functional connectivity between the right parahippocampal gyrus and the temporal pole. Such findings merely mark the beginning of MRI studies that will help discern anatomic corollaries of psychotic-like experiences in cannabis users, as schizophrenia involves many brain regions.

Du Y, Fryer SL, Fu Z, Lin D, Sui J, Chen J, Damaraju E, Mennigen E, Stuart B, Loewy RL, Mathalon DH, Calhoun VD. "Dynamic functional connectivity impairments in early schizophrenia and clinical high-risk for psychosis." *Neuroimage* 180, part B (Oct 15, 2018): 632-645. https://doi.org/10.1016/j.neuroimage.2017.10.022. Epub 2017 Oct 14. PMID: 29038030; PMCID: PMC5899692. https://www.ncbi.nlm.nih.gov/pmc/articles/PMC5899692/pdf/nihms917676.pdf.

Yu T, Jia T, Zhu L, Desrivières S, Macare C, Bi Y, et al. IMAGEN Consortium. "Cannabis- Associated Psychotic-like Experiences Are Mediated by Developmental Changes in the Parahippocampal Gyrus." *J Am Acad Child Adolesc Psychiatry* 59, no. 5 (May 2020): 642-649. https://doi.

org/10.1016/j.jaac.2019.05.034. Epub 2019 Jul 18. PMID: 31326579. https://www.sciencedirect.com/science/article/abs/pii/S0890856719304691.

iv. **A plausible mechanism involving gene-environment interactions and coherence with what is known about genetic risk for psychosis.** That there is a genetic component to schizophrenia is well established from studies showing how risk level is proportional to degree of relatedness to the affected individual (Gottesman and Shields, 1967). The potential for interactions between whatever those genes are and environmental factors is incontrovertible from well-accepted biological principles. Here, the environmental factor in question is cannabis, and there are reports that specific genes or combinations of genes may interact with cannabis use to augment risk for psychosis, even though they may not have led to psychosis in most carriers who were not cannabis users. For example, a "C" allele of AKT1 was determined by Di Forti et al. (2012) to be significantly more prevalent in first- episode psychosis patients who were cannabis users as compared to psychosis patients who were not users. Unfortunately, the ethnic matching between cases and controls was poor, and the adjustment for the differing ethnic frequencies in the genetic marker of interest does not solve the problem (for a discussion of this Issue, see Oetjens et al., 2016). A subsequent AKT1 study in subjects with no family history of psychosis (Morgan et al., 2016) also found a significant association between the AKTI "C" allele and risk for developing psychotic symptoms after cannabis administration under controlled conditions in the clinic, including a strong trend for an effect of ethnicity on the occurrence of the symptoms. Confirmation of the study results would be helpful, in particular because the sign of the standardized regression "β"coefficient for AKT1 does not match that of the raw regression coefficient in Table 2A, an inexplicable result for which no erratum was issued.

A different approach involving multiple genes contributing to what is known as a "polygenic risk score" (PRS) appears promising when applied to a large, ethnically uniform group of subjects. Wainberg et al. (2021) found that frequent cannabis use interacted with the PRS for schizophrenia to significantly augment specific psychotic features (most notably delusions of reference) as compared to PRS gene carriers who did not frequently use cannabis.

In addition to AKT1 and PRS genes, candidate genes predicted to interact with THC from work in animal models have the potential to explain a portion of the gene-environment interactions. For example: 1) genes for receptors that bind THC and have been shown to mediate THC's effect on dopaminergic tone in an animal model; 2) genes for enzymes involved in metabolizing THC and responding to its metabolites; or 3) genes involved in the effect of THC on kynurenine pathway metabolites (see Element 6, parts i and ii above), some of which could theoretically pose risk solely through interaction with cannabis use.

Genetic studies have also been interpreted to undermine cannabis use as being a significant independent risk factor for the general population. A recent study by Kendler et al. (2019) demonstrated that the family history of psychosis was statistically equivalent between cannabis-related schizophrenia cases and typical schizophrenia cases from the general population.

What this and some prior studies of family history failed to do, however, was to determine whether the psychosis cases in the family trees had any association with cannabis or other drug use, which would obviously confound the magnitude of the genetic contribution to psychosis in the group under study.

Yet other genetic association publications point to an overlap between the polygenic risk markers for schizophrenia and polygenic risk markers for lifetime cannabis use (e.g., Pasman et al., 2018). This could be interpreted to signify that the association between the two disorders may not be causal but instead result from the coincidence of the two disorders having the same genes of risk rather than deriving from a gene-environment interaction.

However, the Pasman et al. study was heavily criticized for not actually ascertaining a diagnosis in the subjects labeled as having schizophrenia (Erratum in Nature Neuroscience) and, regardless, the PRS for schizophrenia generally explains only a small percentage of "all cause" schizophrenia patients (Laursen et al., 2017), particularly so for the genes covered by Pasman et al. (3.4 %). Furthermore, other research groups have reported that the schizophrenia-PRS genetic signal in cannabis-using controls was not significantly different than in controls who were non-users (unpublished data in a reply to author, Di Forti et al., 2015), a finding confirmed by the work of Hjorthøj et al. (2021), who found no significant evidence for an association between a high schizophrenia-PRS signal and the development of a cannabis use disorder in otherwise normal controls. And a recent genome-wide meta- analysis of markers for cannabis use disorder identified only a modest correlation between individual genetic markers of risk for cannabis use disorder and schizophrenia (Figure 2, Johnson et al., 2021). In addition, schizophrenia was not one of the 12 mental disorders found to be significantly associated with the PRS genes for cannabis use disorder.

For these reasons, and because only a minority of individuals who develop schizophrenia have a first- or second-degree family history of psychosis (see Element 3 ii above), gene- environment interactions will continue to have merit as a mechanism worthy of exploration. But the genes identified as having the strongest interaction may not have been manifest in a family history of psychosis absent cannabis use and will likely not be genes that predispose to cannabis use.

Di Forti M, Iyegbe C, Sallis H, Kolliakou A, Falcone MA, Paparelli A, Sirianni M, La Cascia C, Stilo SA, Marques TR, Handley R, Mondelli V, Dazzan P, Pariante C, David AS, Morgan C, Powell J, Murray RM. "Confirmation that the AKT1 (rs2494732) genotype influences the risk of psychosis in cannabis users." *Biol Psychiatry* 72, no. 10 (Nov 15, 2012): 811-16. https://doi.org/10.1016/j.biopsych.2012.06.020. Epub 2012 Jul 24. PMID: 22831980. https://pubmed.ncbi.nlm.nih.gov/22831980/.

Di Forti M, Vassos E, Lynskey M, Craig M, Murray RM. "Cannabis and psychosis – Authors' reply." *The Lancet Psychiatry* 2, no. 5 (May 2015): 382. https://doi.org/10.1016/S2215-0366(15)00177-7. Epub 2015 Apr 28. PMID: 26360275. https://www.thelancet.com/journals/lanpsy/article/PIIS2215-0366%2815%2900177-7/fulltext.

Gottesman II, Shields J. "A polygenic theory of schizophrenia." *Proc Natl Acad Sci U S A* 58, no. 1 (Jul 1967): 199-205. https://doi.org/10.1073/pnas.58.1.199. PMID: 5231600; PMCID: PMC335617. https://www.ncbi.nlm.nih.gov/pmc/articles/PMC335617/pdf/pnas00677-0218.pdf.

Hjorthøj C, Uddin MJ, Wimberley T, Dalsgaard S, Hougaard DM, Børglum A, Werge T, Nordentoft M. "No evidence of associations between genetic liability for schizophrenia and development of cannabis use disorder." *Psychol Med.* 51, no. 3 (Feb 2021): 479-484. https://doi.org/10.1017/S0033291719003362. Epub 2019 Dec 9. PMID: 31813396. https://pubmed.ncbi.nlm.nih.gov/31813396/.

Johnson EC, Demontis D, Thorgeirsson TE, Walters RK, Polimanti R, Hatoum AS. "A large-scale genome-wide association study meta-analysis of cannabis use disorder." *The Lancet Psychiatry* 7, no. 12 (Dec 2020): 1032-1045. https://doi.org/10.1016/S2215-0366(20)30339-4. Epub 2020 Oct 20. PMID: 33096046; PMCID: PMC7674631. https://www.thelancet.com/action/showPdf?pii=S2215-0366%2820%2930339-4.

Kendler KS, Ohlsson H, Sundquist J, Sundquist K. "Prediction of Onset of Substance-Induced Psychotic Disorder and Its Progression to Schizophrenia in a Swedish National Sample." *Am J Psychiatry* 176, no. 9 (Sep 1, 2019): 711-719. https://doi.org/10.1176/appi.ajp.2019.18101217. Epub 2019 May 6. PMID: 31055966; PMCID: PMC6718312. https://www.ncbi.nlm.nih.gov/pmc/articles/PMC6718312/pdf/nihms-1525260.pdf.

Laursen TM, Trabjerg BB, Mors O, Børglum AD, Hougaard DM, Mattheisen M, Meier SM, Byrne EM, Mortensen PB, Munk-Olsen T, Agerbo E. "Association of the polygenic risk score for schizophrenia with mortality and suicidal behavior – A Danish population-based study." *Schizophr Res.* 184 (Jun 2017): 122-127. https://doi.org/10.1016/j.schres.2016.12.001. Epub 2016 Dec 6. PMID: 27939829. https://pubmed.ncbi.nlm.nih.gov/27939829/.

Morgan CJ, Freeman TP, Powell J, Curran HV. "AKT1 genotype moderates the acute psychotomimetic effects of naturalistically smoked cannabis in young cannabis smokers." *Transl Psychiatry* 6, no. 2 (Feb 2016): e738. https://doi.org/10.1038/tp.2015.219. PMID: 26882038; PMCID: PMC4872423. https://www.ncbi.nlm.nih.gov/pmc/articles/PMC4872423/pdf/tp2015219a.pdf.

Oetjens MT, Brown-Gentry K, Goodloe R, Dilks HH, Crawford DC. "Population Stratification in the Context of Diverse Epidemiologic Surveys

Sans Genome-Wide Data." *Front. Genet.* 7, no. 76 (May 6, 2016). https://doi.org/10.3389/fgene.2016.00076. PMID: 27200085; PMCID: PMC4858524. https://www.ncbi.nlm.nih.gov/pmc/articles/PMC4858524/pdf/fgene-07-00076.pdf.

Pasman JA, Verweij KJH, Gerring Z, Stringer S, Sanchez-Roige S, Treur JL, et al. "GWAS of lifetime cannabis use reveals new risk loci, genetic overlap with psychiatric traits, and a causal influence of schizophrenia." *Nat Neurosci.* 21, no. 9 (Sep 2018): 1161-1170. https://doi.org/10.1038/s41593-018-0206-1. Epub 2018 Aug 27. Erratum in: *Nat Neurosci.* 22, no. 7 (Jul 2019): 1196. PMID: 30150663; PMCID: PMC6386176. https://www.ncbi.nlm.nih.gov/pmc/articles/PMC6386176/pdf/nihms-1003328.pdf.

Wainberg M, Jacobs GR, Di Forti M, Tripathy SJ. "Cannabis, schizophrenia genetic risk, and psychotic experiences: a cross-sectional study of 109,308 participants from the UK Biobank." *Transl Psychiatry* 11, no. 1 (Apr 9, 2021): 211. https://doi.org/10.1038/s41398-021-01330-w. PMID: 33837184; PMCID: PMC8035271. https://www.ncbi.nlm.nih.gov/pmc/articles/PMC8035271/pdf/41398_2021_Article_1330.pdf.

7. Experimental evidence (obtained under controlled conditions where cause and effect are more easily discerned).

i. When studied in controlled clinical settings, a moderate dose of the active ingredient in cannabis (THC) elicits transient psychotic symptoms in normal cohort-controlled subjects with no family history of psychosis, and an increase in the average PANSS, a well-accepted clinical assessment tool to measure positive and negative symptoms of psychosis.

D'Souza DC, Perry E, MacDougall L, Ammerman Y, Cooper T, Wu YT, Braley G, Gueorguieva R, Krystal JH. "The Psychotomimetic Effects of Intravenous Delta-9-Tetrahydrocannabinol in Healthy Individuals: Implications for Psychosis." *Neuropsychopharmacology* 29, no. 8 (Aug 2004): 1558-72. https://www.nature.com/articles/1300496.pdf.

Freeman D, Dunn G, Murray RM, Evans N, Lister R, Antley A, Slater M, Godlewska B, Cornish R, Williams J, Di Simplicio M, Igoumenou A, Brenneisen R, Tunbridge EM, Harrison PJ, Harmer CJ, Cowen P, Morrison PD. "How Cannabis Causes Paranoia: Using the Intravenous Administration of Δ^9-Tetrahydrocannabinol (THC) to Identify Key Cognitive Mechanisms Leading to Paranoia." *Schizophr Bull.* 41, no. 2 (2015): 391-9. https://www.ncbi.nlm.nih.gov/pmc/articles/PMC4332941/pdf/sbu098.pdf.

Morrison PD, Nottage J, Stone JM, Bhattacharyya S, Tunstall N, Brenneisen R, Holt D, Wilson D, Sumich A, McGuire P, Murray RM, Kapur S, Ffytche DH. "Disruption of Frontal Theta Coherence by Δ^9-Tetrahydrocannabinol Is Associated with Positive Psychotic Symptoms." *Neuropsychopharmacology* 36, no. 4 (2011): 827-36. https://www.ncbi.nlm.nih.gov/pmc/articles/PMC3055738/pdf/npp2010222a.pdf.

    ii.   Two studies reported the percentage of subjects that experienced psychotic symptoms, specifically 40% of subjects (Morrison et al., 2011, and see figure 2 of Bhattacharyya et al., 2012).

Bhattacharyya S, Crippa JA, Allen P, Martin-Santos R, Borgwardt S, Fusar-Poli P, Rubia K, Kambeitz J, O'Carroll C, Seal ML, Giampietro V, Brammer M, Zuardi AW, Atakan Z, McGuire PK. "Induction of Psychosis by Δ9-Tetrahydrocannabinol Reflects Modulation of Prefrontal and Striatal Function During Attentional Salience Processing." *Arch Gen Psychiatry* 69, no. 1 (2012): 27-36. https://jamanetwork.com/journals/jamapsychiatry/fullarticle/1107444.

Morrison PD, Nottage J, Stone JM, Bhattacharyya S, Tunstall N, Brenneisen R, Holt D, Wilson D, Sumich A, McGuire P, Murray RM, Kapur S, Ffytche DH. "Disruption of Frontal Theta Coherence by Δ^9-Tetrahydrocannabinol Is Associated with Positive Psychotic Symptoms." *Neuropsychopharmacology* 36, no. 4 (2011): 827-36. https://www.ncbi.nlm.nih.gov/pmc/articles/PMC3055738/pdf/npp2010222a.pdf.

8. Analogous evidence (If something similar to A causes something similar to B, then A likely causes B).

This condition is satisfied by the observation that other drugs of abuse that increase dopamine release in the brain (Koob and Volkow, 2016) are capable of resulting in a chronic psychotic disorder similar to that caused by cannabis (Niemi-Pyntarri et al., 2013; Starzer et al., 2017). The experimental findings in section 8 are also relevant, because in the clinic, THC elicits a precursor to chronic psychotic disorders (psychotic symptoms); therefore, THC should also cause chronic psychotic disorders.

Koob GF, Volkow ND. "Neurobiology of addiction: a neurocircuitry analysis." *The Lancet Psychiatry* 3, no. 8 (Aug 2016): 760-773. https://doi.org/10.1016/S2215-0366(16)00104-8. PMID: 27475769; PMCID: PMC6135092. https://www.ncbi.nlm.nih.gov/pmc/articles/PMC6135092/pdf/nihms-985499.pdf.

Niemi-Pynttäri JA, Sund R, Putkonen H, Vorma H, Wahlbeck K, Pirkola SP. "Substance-Induced Psychoses Converting into Schizophrenia: A Register-Based Study of 18,478 Finnish Inpatient Cases." *J Clin Psychiatry* 74, no. 1 (2013): e94-9. https://www.psychiatrist.com/jcp/article/Pages/2013/v74n01/v74n0115.aspx.

Starzer MSK, Nordentoft M, Hjorthøj C. "Rates and Predictors of Conversion to Schizophrenia or Bipolar Disorder Following Substance-Induced Psychosis." *Am J Psychiatry* 175, no. 4 (2018): 343-50. https://ajp. psychiatryonline.org/doi/abs/10.1176/appi.ajp.2017.17020223?rfr_dat=cr_pub%3Dpu bmed&url_ver=Z39.88-2003&rfr_id=ori%3Arid%3Acrossref. org&journalCode=ajp.

Conclusion

The currently available research on cannabis causing chronic psychotic disorders satisfies the Bradford Hill elements of causation. This means that some people who develop a chronic psychotic disorder after using cannabis would not have developed the disorder had they not used cannabis. Even if a certain amount of residual confounding remains, for example unquantified variations in other environmental risks or in genetic background, it is not enough to undermine the effect of cannabis as an independent risk factor.

APPENDIX 2

Applying the Bradford Hill Criteria for Causation to the Relationship Between Marijuana Use and Suicidal Behavior

By Christine L. Miller, PhD September 2020

In 1965, Sir Bradford Hill developed a set of tests designed to elucidate causal relationships in epidemiology. These criteria have subsequently become accepted as important standards for epidemiological and clinical science, as reviewed by van Reekum et al. (2001) for neuropsychiatry applications.

1. Demonstration of a strong association between the causative agent and the outcome (author's note: often termed "correlation," it is the first criteria required to be satisfied for causation): √

Among the largest effect sizes for increased risk of suicide *attempt* in marijuana users were found in two longitudinal studies of predominantly White youth, both of which adjusted for a variety of potentially confounding factors. One study combined 3 longitudinal data sets involving 6 to 9 assessments over a period of 15 years, finding a 6.9-fold increase in risk for subsequent suicide attempt in those using marijuana daily before age 17 (Silins et al., 2014). As well as adjusting for measures of depression and conduct disorder, along with a variety of demographics, the adjustment factors specific to other drug use included tobacco use, alcohol use, and other illicit drug use. The second longitudinal study with a large effect size included two assessments and a follow-up time of 8 years (Clarke et al., 2014). It was notable in that it adjusted for a history of any mood disorder (including depression), in addition to familial/adolescent risk factors and alcohol use, but not tobacco or other drug use, finding a 7.5-fold increase in risk for suicide attempt when the marijuana use commenced in the teen years.

As the best predictor of completed suicide is suicide attempt (Nordstrom et al., 1995; Hawton et al., 2013), it would be expected that the increased risk would be fairly similar in magnitude for suicide attempt and completed suicides. Indeed, a 2013 study of predominantly Caucasian subjects found a 5.3-fold increased risk for completed suicide in those with a cannabis use disorder (Arendt et al., 2013). Although a variety of demographic and personal risk factors were adjusted for, other substance use was only available for the month before cannabis abuse treatment commenced.

2. Consistency of the findings across research sites and methodologies: √

A meta-analysis of a mix of longitudinal and case-control studies worldwide, some including a mix of ethnic groups (African ancestry, Hispanic ancestry) with a lower risk of suicide than Caucasians (Curtin et al., 2016), found an overall 2.2-fold increase in risk for suicide attempt in users of marijuana, a 3.2-fold increased risk of suicide attempt in heavy users, and a 2.6-fold increase in risk for completed suicides in ever users (Borges et al., 2016). The follow-up times in the longitudinal studies ranged from 1 year to 33 years, averaging somewhat less than 7 years.

There have been only a few reports that failed to find an association, including a case-control (no follow-up) study of 9,268 Swiss adolescents (Gex et al., 1998). Given the study size, the lack of follow-up limited the sensitivity of the study, and the investigators found no association between suicide attempt and marijuana use after controlling for a variety of potentially confounding variables, including tobacco smoking. Because many marijuana users during that general time period also began smoking tobacco if they were not already smokers (Patton et al., 2005), correcting for tobacco use would be expected to substantially reduce the effect size of marijuana and, therefore, could potentially explain the lack of association found depending on the study power. In a study of other mental health outcomes in 50,087 Swedish conscripts by Zammit et al. (2002), 86% of the marijuana users also smoked cigarettes. In the same cohort, Price (2009) found that an unadjusted 1.6-fold increase in risk for completed suicide in the 33-year longitudinal study was eliminated after adjusting for confounding variables, including smoking of tobacco. Although the total study population was quite large, the small number of completed suicides expected in the cannabis-using group (likely <30), means statistical power may have been quite limited after adjustments for confounding variables. Suicide attempts are much more frequent and afford greater statistical power. A longitudinal study of suicide attempts by Rasic et al. (2013) in a cohort of 976 Canadian high school students over a two-year period, found that marijuana users were more likely to be depressed after adjusting for other illicit drug use and alcohol (but apparently not tobacco), but were not significantly more likely to attempt suicide than nonusers. Notably, this study was underpowered to detect anything less than a 2.7-fold effect of marijuana on suicide attempt (a smaller increase in risk would certainly be of interest, particularly since the two-year follow-up period was so short).

The evidence for tobacco use confounding the association of marijuana with suicide risk is strong (Miller et al., 2011; Bohnert et al., 2014; Evins et al., 2017). Yet, after decades of tobacco prevention education, the use of tobacco by US youth began to decline (Centers for Disease Control, 2020), as well as use by all age groups worldwide (WHO, 2019), while marijuana-only use has increased (Schauer and Peters, 2018) to the extent that it became easier for researchers to investigate marijuana-specific effects independent of cigarette use.

In a recent case-control study (Kahn and Wilcox, 2020) of a large (59,079) ethnically mixed population of US high school students, adjusting for a variety of factors as well as tobacco and alcohol use, revealed that the impact of marijuana on suicide attempts was still significant, with an enhanced prevalence of suicide attempt of 2.6-fold for those who used marijuana 20 or more days per month and at that same rate of use, a 4.5-fold enhanced prevalence of suicide attempts requiring medical intervention. There was no follow-up in this study of incident marijuana use and suicidal behaviors over one year, and for the studies reviewed by Borges et al. (2016), the follow-up was on average shorter than the Silins et al. and Clarke et al. studies mentioned above showing higher impact. Kahn et al. also reported that marijuana use was generally equivalent to the impacts of tobacco and alcohol; however, this proportionality might not persist in a longitudinal study because the relative impact of each substance could theoretically change as more of those attempting suicide are registered over time in a cohort population.

3. Demonstration of specificity of the causative agent in terms of the outcomes it produces: N/A (see van Reekum et al., 2001)

This criterion may be applicable to outcomes from infectious organisms to a certain extent, but is not considered applicable to neuropsychiatry and neuropharmacology (van Reekum et al., 2001), where one drug can result in many different outcomes and, conversely, many different drugs are associated with suicidal behavior, including tobacco products, alcohol (Kahn and Wilcox, 2020), and other recreational drugs of abuse (reviewed by Miller, 2018).

4. Demonstration of the appropriate temporal sequence so that the causative agent occurs prior to the outcome: +/-

More work needs to be done on the timing of marijuana use and suicide, although the existing data is strongly suggestive of an appropriate temporal sequence in some, but not all, studies. For this criterion, longitudinal studies are the most important. Of those identified with adequate assessment intervals and time frame, one (also described above) involved the analysis of 3 separate longitudinal studies combined, totaling 2,675 predominantly Caucasian youth starting at age 16 for each study, with follow-up through age 30, as reported by Silins et al. (2014). Yearly assessments were conducted (with mental health data prior to age 16 acquired retrospectively), numerous potentially confounding variables were adjusted for, and for those youth who were using marijuana daily by the age of 17, the risk of suicide attempt over the ensuing years was found to be significantly increased (6.9-fold) as compared to controls.

A subsequent meta-analysis of only longitudinal studies assessing marijuana use that commenced at ages less than 18 years (Gobbi et al., 2019), identified a significant 3.46-fold increase in risk for suicide attempt during young adulthood in those with no pre-existing suicidal behaviors, depression, or anxiety. Not all of the included studies adjusted for other drugs of abuse, use of tobacco cigarettes, or psychosocial factors.

A third longitudinal analysis found no significant impact of marijuana on suicide attempt (Agrawal et al., 2017), utilizing a database that assessed an ethnically mixed group of 3,277 subjects (30% African American, 70% Caucasian) every two years over a period of 10 years, and encompassed a large age range at study inception, ages 12 to 22. Even early marijuana use (<15 yrs. of age) was not significantly associated with subsequent suicide attempt; however, the study was underpowered to detect less than a 1.5-fold increase in risk. Intriguingly, a prior history of suicidal ideation was significantly protective for initiating marijuana use, while prior suicide attempts had no impact on initiating marijuana, though lack of statistical power would have influenced the latter result. Unlike the Silins et al. study, they did not investigate the effect of frequency of use on later suicide attempts. The study adjusted for race, but it did not report a separate analysis for Caucasians alone.

Yet, a recent data summary of case reports, with no statistical analysis, found that for 303 adults (aged 18 and over) with a self-reported history of marijuana use admitted over a 4-month period to the Emergency Department of an urban hospital (Marco et al., 2020), 9% had experienced suicidal ideation in the past 30 days (whereas 2.4% has been reported as the one month prevalence in the adult population by Olfson et al., 1998, and 4.6% as the one month prevalence for teens, Turner et al., 2012), and most strikingly, of the 41% who had experienced lifetime suicidal ideation, the timing of their marijuana initiation preceded the onset of suicidal ideation in the vast majority of cases (91%). Of note, the majority did not perceive any harm associated with their use and, therefore, were not attempting to excuse mental health problems by revealing marijuana use. Suicidal ideation, however, is not as strong a predictor of subsequent suicide as is a suicide attempt (McHugh et al., 2019; Nordstrom et al., 1995; Hawton et al., 2013). No statistical analysis nor correction for potentially confounding variables was carried out. The subjects were a fairly balanced mix of Caucasians and African Americans, with a small percentage of Hispanics and other groups.

Rather than limiting the analysis to a direct effect of marijuana use on subsequent suicidal behavior, the effect of marijuana to trigger mental health disorders (major depression, bipolar disorder, and schizophrenia; Miller, 2018) must be evaluated as an indirect mechanism leading to risk for suicide, because such disorders are associated with a much greater risk (7 to 21-fold) during the early stages of illness, even in the absence of marijuana use (Randall et al., 2014).

Nussbaum et al. (2011) published a case report concerning a patient whose depression surfaced after marijuana use began at age 18, eventually leading to polydrug use. In the weeks before the patient's suicide attempt, it was her marijuana use that doubled. For such indirect cases, the temporal sequence would nevertheless be satisfied.

Finally, there is some evidence that marijuana can exert an acute effect to increase suicide risk in the short term, where the temporal sequence is clearer. In such cases, the acute effect of marijuana may be more similar to alcohol (Kaplan et al., 2013) than to tobacco (Kassel et al., 2007). Although rates of lifetime suicidal ideation or suicide attempts can be surprisingly high (e.g., Agrawal et al., 2017), the acute risk on any particular day for the general population remains very low; therefore, reports of a temporal sequence of events over a few days or on the same day carry more meaning. Among marijuana-using teens (68% Caucasian), use of marijuana on a particular day is reported to be a predictor of a suicide attempt on that day (Sellers et al., 2019). Lacking more extensive longitudinal research on the issue, case reports and anecdotal evidence can also offer some important insights. Suicidal ideation was observed in one out of fourteen subjects administered a liquid form of pure Δ9-THC (20 mg doses) over a period of 3 days in a clinical setting (Gorelick et al., 2011). Russo et al. (2015) observed the onset of suicidal ideation in a patient treating the spasticity of multiple sclerosis with a formulation containing Δ9-THC. Multiple sclerosis patients are already at higher risk for suicide, and a similar impact of Δ9-THC has been observed in other cases (Langford et al., 2013). Koppel et al. (2014) review reports of suicidal ideation following medical use of cannabinoids. Episodic marijuana use in a patient was found to result in acute suicidal ideation only during the periods of use (Raja and Azzoni, 2009), with a return to normalcy in the intervals of non-use. A Centers for Disease Control MMWR report attributes the intentional and fatal jump of a young college student from a hotel balcony to his recent consumption of a potent marijuana edible (Centers for Disease Control, July 24, 2015). The anecdotal report of a *New York Times* columnist (Dowd, 2014) describes overwhelming feelings of impending doom that lasted for hours after consumption of a potent marijuana candy bar during her 2014 visit to Colorado, and such feelings could be expected to lead to suicidal urges in those less able to mentally cope. Following Dowd's experience, a young, seemingly very well-adjusted college graduate visiting Keystone in 2016 to ski with his cousin, killed himself after consuming too many marijuana edibles, as reported by Michael Roberts in *Westword* (March 26, 2015). Roberts also covered the self-stabbing death of Daniel Juarez, who was intoxicated from high levels of Δ9-THC in his system, and the suicide of Brant Clark, which occurred a few weeks after he experienced a psychotic break from marijuana use (Roberts, May 19, 2015).

5. Demonstration of a biological gradient, in which more of the causative agent leads to a poorer outcome: √

Here, the studies looking at frequency of use show greatest impact with higher use rates (daily use most impactful, inferred from Silins et al., 2014; "heavy use" of greater impact than ever-use in a meta-analysis by Borges et al., 2016). Kahn and Wilcox (2020) provide a more fine-tuned investigation of the impact of frequency of use, investigating marijuana use rates of 1–2, 3–9, 10–19, and 20+ use days per month, and finding an enhanced prevalence of suicide attempt (as compared to nonusers) of 1.65, 2.11, 2.13, and 2.64-fold respectively. The corresponding figures for suicide attempt requiring medical intervention were 1.98, 2.52, 3.15, and 4.51-fold.

6. Demonstration of a biologic rationale, such that it makes sense that the suspected agent causes the outcome: √

Bloomfield et al. (2016) reviewed the overall experimental evidence that Δ9-THC stimulates the

dopaminergic reward system of the brain, and over time, depletes the integrity of the system leading to exhaustion of dopaminergic tone. As this reward system is important to deriving pleasure from everyday life, it is understandable that chronic use of THC may lead to a loss of interest in continuing to live. Several drugs of abuse act on the dopamine reward system (Blum et al., 2015).

7. Coherence of the findings, such that the causation argument is in agreement with what we already know: √

Suicide causation is almost always multifactorial (Pandey, 2013; Vijayakumar et al., 2016) and rarely associated with a single cause; therefore, this criterion is satisfied as it is consistent with what is known about other suspected causes, i.e., the impact of chronic marijuana use is thought to be exerted primarily in conjunction with other factors.

8. Experimental evidence: √

As stated above: "Suicidal ideation was observed in one out of fourteen subjects administered a liquid form of pure Δ9-THC (20 mg doses) over a period of 3 days in a clinical setting (Gorelick et al., 2011). Subjects at already higher risk for suicide may similarly show a temporal relationship between suicidal ideation and administration of formulations containing Δ9-THC (Langford et al., 2013). Koppel et al. (2014) review reports of suicidal ideation following medical use of cannabinoids."

9. Evidence from analogous conditions: N/A (see van Reekum et al., 2001)

For neuropsychiatric outcomes, parallels between related neuropsychiatric conditions is not a necessary finding because the response of the brain to different insults is so complex.

Conclusions

All but one (#4) of the seven relevant Bradford Hill criteria have been satisfied for the causal connection between marijuana use and the development of suicidal behavior. The evidence that an "appropriate temporal sequence" exists (outlined in criterion #4) is strongly suggestive though remains unconfirmed from an academic standpoint. Further study is required in the form of longitudinal studies that are prospective in nature. Adequate length of follow-up time and number of assessment intervals, ability to adjust effectively for polysubstance use with respect to timing of use, distinguishing acute from chronic effects, addressing ethnic diversity with respect to outcome, and ensuring adequate statistical power should be incorporated in future research paradigms.

Nevertheless, the weight of the evidence currently available should be regarded as strong enough to elicit widespread public health warnings about the suspected role of marijuana use in precipitating suicidal behaviors, since the mandate of the relevant authorities is to err on the side of protecting public health rather than to establish scientific certainty beyond a shadow of a doubt. This is particularly urgent in view of the continuing increase in completed suicides in conjunction with rising marijuana-use rates and more potent products, not only in specific states but across the nation as a whole (Miller et al., 2020).

REFERENCES

Agrawal A, Nelson EC, Bucholz KK, Tillman R, Grucza RA, Statham DJ, Madden PA, Martin NG, Heath AC, Lynskey MT. "Major Depressive Disorder, Suicidal Thoughts and Behaviors, and Cannabis Involvement in Discordant Twins: a Retrospective Cohort Study. *The Lancet Psychiatry* 4, no. 9 (2017): 706-714.

https://www.ncbi.nlm.nih.gov/pmc/articles/PMC5696002/pdf/nihms896582.pdf.

Arendt M, Munk-Jørgensen P, Sher L, Jensen SO. "Mortality following treatment for cannabis use disorders: predictors and causes." *J Subst Abuse Treat.* 44, no. 4 (2013): 400-406. https://www.journalofsubstanceabusetreatment.com/article/S0740-5472(12)00382-0/fulltext.

Bloomfield MA, Ashok AH, Volkow ND, Howes OD. "The effects of Δ9-tetrahydrocannabinol on the dopamine system." *Nature* 539, no. 7629 (2016): 369-77. https://www.ncbi.nlm.nih.gov/pmc/articles/PMC5123717/pdf/emss-70462.pdf.

Blum K, Thanos PK, Oscar-Berman M, Febo M, Baron D, Badgaiyan RD, Gardner E, Demetrovics Z, Fahlke C, Haberstick BC, Dushaj K, Gold MS. "Dopamine in the Brain: Hypothesizing Surfeit or Deficit Links to Reward and Addiction." *J Reward Defic Syndr.* 1, no. 3 (2015): 95-104.

https://www.ncbi.nlm.nih.gov/pmc/articles/PMC4936401/pdf/nihms-748853.pdf.

Bohnert KM, Ilgen MA, McCarthy JF, Ignacio RV, Blow FC, Katz IR. "Tobacco use disorder and the risk of suicide mortality." *Addiction* 109, no. 1 (2014): 155-62. https://deepblue.lib.umich.edu/bitstream/handle/2027.42/102156/add12381.pdf?sequence=1&is Allowed=y.

Borges G, Bagge CL, Orozco R. "A literature review and meta-analyses of cannabis use and suicidality." *J Affect Disord.* 195 (2016): 63-74. https://www.sciencedirect.com/science/article/abs/pii/S0165032715310004?via%3Dihub.

Centers for Disease Control (CDC). Morbidity and Mortality Weekly Report (MMWR), *Notes from the Field: Death Following Ingestion of an Edible Marijuana Product—Colorado, March 2014*, July 24, 2015. https://www.cdc.gov/mmwr/preview/mmwrhtml/mm6428a6.htm.

Centers for Disease Control (CDC). Youth Risk Behavior Survey, *Trends in the Prevalence of Tobacco Use National YRBS: 1991—2019*, last reviewed August 20, 2020. https://www.cdc.gov/healthyyouth/data/yrbs/factsheets/2019_tobacco_trend_yrbs.htm.

Clarke MC, Coughlan H, Harley M, Connor D, Power E, Lynch F, et al. "The impact of adolescent cannabis use, mood disorder and lack of education on attempted suicide in young adulthood." *World Psychiatry* 13, no. 3 (2014):322-323. https://europepmc.org/backend/ptpmcrender.fcgi?accid=PMC4219077&blobtype=pdf.

Curtin SC, Warner M, Hedegaard H. "Suicide Rates for Females and Males by Race and Ethnicity: United States, 1999 and 2014." Centers for Disease Control and Prevention, National Center for Health Statistics E-Stats, Hyattsville, MD, April 2016. https://www.cdc.gov/nchs/data/hestat/suicide/rates_1999_2014.htm.

Dowd M, "Don't Harsh Our Mellow, Dude," *The New York Times*, June 3, 2014, http://www.nytimes.com/2014/06/04/opinion/dowd-dont-harsh-our-mellow-dude.html.

Evins AE, Korhonen T, Kinnunen TH, Kaprio J. "Prospective association between tobacco smoking and death by suicide: a competing risks hazard analysis in a large twin cohort with 35- year follow-up." *Psychol Med.* 47, no. 12 (2017): 2143-2154. https://www.ncbi.nlm.nih.gov/pmc/articles/PMC5551385/pdf/S0033291717000587a.pdf.

Gex CR, Narring F, Ferron C, Michaud P. "Suicide attempts among adolescents in Switzerland: prevalence, associated factors and comorbidity." *Acta Psychiatrica Scandinavica* 98, no. 1 (1998): 28-33.

https://onlinelibrary.wiley.com/doi/abs/10.1111/j.1600-0447.1998.tb10038.x.

Gobbi G, Atkin T, Zytynski T, Wang S, Askari S, Boruff J, Ware M, Marmorstein N, Cipriani A, Dendukuri N, Mayo N. "Association of Cannabis Use in Adolescence and Risk of Depression, Anxiety, and Suicidality in Young Adulthood: A Systematic Review and Meta-analysis." *JAMA Psychiatry* 76, no. 4 (2019): 426-434.

https://www.ncbi.nlm.nih.gov/pmc/articles/PMC6450286/.

Gorelick DA, Goodwin RS, Schwilke E, Schwope DM, Darwin WD, Kelly DL, et al. "Antagonist-Elicited Cannabis Withdrawal in Humans." *J Clin Psychopharmacol* 31, no. 5 (2011): 603-12.

https://www.ncbi.nlm.nih.gov/pmc/articles/PMC3717344/pdf/nihms486934.pdf.

Hawton K, Casañas I Comabella C, Haw C, Saunders K. "Risk factors for suicide in individuals with depression: a systematic review." *J Affect Disord.* 147, No. 1–3 (2013): 17-28. https://pubmed.ncbi.nlm.nih.gov/23411024/.

Kahn GD, Wilcox HC. "Marijuana Use Is Associated with Suicidal Ideation and Behavior Among US Adolescents at Rates Similar to Tobacco and Alcohol." *Arch Suicide Res.* (Aug 11, 2020), online ahead of print. https://www.tandfonline.com/doi/full/10.1080/13811118.2020.1804025.

Kaplan MS, McFarland BH, Huguet N, Conner K, Caetano R, Giesbrecht N, Nolte KB. "Acute alcohol intoxication and suicide: a gender-stratified analysis of the National Violent Death Reporting System." *Inj Prev.* 19, no. 1 (2013) :38-43. https://www.ncbi.nlm.nih.gov/pmc/articles/PMC3760342/pdf/nihms-505996.pdf.

Kassel JD, Evatt DP, Greenstein JE, Wardle MC, Yates MC, Veilleux JC. "The acute effects of nicotine on positive and negative affect in adolescent smokers." *J Abnorm Psychol* 116, no. 3 (2007): 543-53. https://pubmed.ncbi.nlm.nih.gov/17696710/.

Koppel BS, Brust JC, Fife T, Bronstein J, Youssof S, Gronseth G, et al. "Systematic review: Efficacy and safety of medical marijuana in selected neurologic disorders – Report of the Guideline Development Subcommittee of the American Academy of Neurology." *Neurology* 82, no. 17 (2014): 1556-63.

https://www.ncbi.nlm.nih.gov/pmc/articles/PMC4011465/pdf/NEUROLOGY2013552075.pdf.

Langford RM, Mares J, Novotna A, Vachova M, Novakova I, Notcutt W, Ratcliffe S. "A double-blind, randomized, placebo-controlled, parallel-group study of THC/CBD oromucosal spray in combination with the existing treatment regimen, in the relief of central neuropathic pain in patients with multiple sclerosis." *J Neurol.* 260, no. 4 (2013): 984-97. https://www.researchgate.net/profile/Stuart_Ratcliffe/publication/233770159_A_double- blind_randomized_placebo-controlled_parallel- group_study_of_THCCBD_oromucosal_spray_in_combination_with_the_existing_treatment_re gimen_in_the_relief_of_central_neuropathic_pain_in_patients_wi/links/57d8111a08ae6399a39912da/A-double-blind-randomized-placebo-controlled-parallel-group-study-of-THC-CBD- oromucosal-spray-in-combination-with-the-existing-treatment-regimen-in-the-relief-of-central- neuropathic-pain-in-patien.pdf.

Marco CA, Detherage JP, LaFountain A, Hannah M, Anderson J, Rhee R, Ziegman J, Mann D. "The perils of recreational marijuana use: relationships with mental health among emergency department patients." *J Am College Emergency Physicians Open* (January 21, 2020), online ahead of print. https://onlinelibrary.wiley.com/doi/epdf/10.1002/emp2.12025.

McHugh CM, Corderoy A, Ryan CJ, Hickie IB, Large MM. "Association between suicidal ideation and suicide: meta-analyses of odds ratios, sensitivity, specificity and positive predictive value." *BJPsych Open* 5 no. 2 (2019): e1. https://www.ncbi.nlm.nih.gov/pmc/articles/PMC6401538/pdf/S2056472418000881a.pdf.

Miller CL. "The Impact of Marijuana on Mental Health" in *Contemporary Health Issues on Marijuana*. Winters K and Sabet K, eds. (Oxford University Press, 2018).

https://global.oup.com/academic/product/contemporary-health-issues-on-marijuana- 9780190263072?q=Contemporary%20Health%20Issues%20on%20Marijuana&lang=en&cc=us.

Miller CL, Jackson MC, Sabet K. "Marijuana and Suicide: Case-control Studies, Population Data, and Potential Neurochemical Mechanisms" in *Cannabis in Medicine, An Evidence-Based Approach*. Finn K, ed. (Springer Press, 2020). https://www.springer.com/fr/book/9783030459673?gclid=EAIaIQobChMIrp_0wfjR6QIVSY2FCh1xfA-ZEAEYASABEgJuX_D_BwE#aboutAuthors.

Miller M, Borges G, Orozco R, Mukamal K, Rimm EB, Benjet C, Medina-Mora ME. "Exposure to alcohol, drugs and tobacco and the risk of subsequent suicidality: findings from the Mexican Adolescent Mental Health Survey. *Drug Alcohol Depend.* 113, no. 2–3 (2011): 110-7. https://www.sciencedirect.com/science/article/abs/pii/S0376871610002620?via%3Dihub.

Nordström P, Asberg M, Aberg-Wistedt A, Nordin C. "Attempted suicide predicts suicide risk in mood disorders." *Acta Psychiatr Scand.* 92, no. 5 (1995) :345-50. https://onlinelibrary.wiley.com/doi/abs/10.1111/j.1600-0447.1995.tb09595.x?sid=nlm%3Apubmed.

Nussbaum A, Thurstone C, Binswanger I. "Medical Marijuana Use and Suicide Attempt in a Patient with Major Depressive Disorder." *Am J Psychiatry* 168, no. 8 (2011): 778-81. https://www.ncbi.nlm.nih.gov/pmc/articles/PMC5242320/pdf/nihms841724.pdf.

Olfson M, Weissman MM, Leon AC, Sheehan DV, Farber L. "Suicidal ideation in primary care." *J Gen Intern Med* 11, no.8 (1996): 447-53.

https://pubmed.ncbi.nlm.nih.gov/8872781/.

Pandey GN. "Biological basis of suicide and suicidal behavior." *Bipolar Disord.* 15, no.5 (2013): 524-41.

https://www.ncbi.nlm.nih.gov/pmc/articles/PMC3749837/pdf/nihms-476618.pdf.

Patton GC, Coffey C, Carlin JB, Sawyer SM, Lynskey M. "Reverse gateways? Frequent cannabis use as a predictor of tobacco initiation and nicotine dependence." *Addiction* 100, no.10 (2005): 1518- 25.

https://onlinelibrary.wiley.com/doi/
abs/10.1111/j.1360-0443.2005.01220.x?sid=nlm%3Apubmed.

Price C, Hemmingsson T, Lewis G, Zammit S, Allebeck P. "Cannabis
and suicide: longitudinal study." *Br J Psychiatry* 195, no. 6 (2009): 492-7.
https://pubmed.ncbi.nlm.nih.gov/19949196/.

Raja M, Azzoni A. "Suicidal Ideation Induced by Episodic Cannabis Use.
Case Report." *Med*. 2009, article ID 321456.

https://www.ncbi.nlm.nih.gov/pmc/articles/PMC2729295/pdf/
CRM2009-321456.pdf.

Randall JR, Walld R, Finlayson G, Sareen J, Martens PJ, Bolton JM.
"Acute Risk of Suicide and Suicide Attempts Associated with Recent
Diagnosis of Mental Disorders: A Population-Based, Propensity Score-
Matched Analysis." *Can J Psychiatry* 59, no. 10 (Oct 2014): 531-8. https://
www.ncbi.nlm.nih.gov/pmc/articles/PMC4197787/pdf/cjp-2014-vol59-
october-531- 538.pdf.

Rasic D, Weerasinghe S, Asbridge M, Langille DB. "Longitudinal
associations of cannabis and illicit drug use with depression,
suicidal ideation and suicidal attempts among Nova Scotia high
school students." *Drug and Alcohol Dependence* 129, no. 1–2 (2013):
49-53. https://www.sciencedirect.com/science/article/abs/pii/
S0376871612003730?via%3Dihub.

Roberts M, "Luke Goodman Killed Himself in Keystone Because of Pot
Edibles, Family Says," *Westword*, March 26, 2015.

https://www.westword.com/news/luke-goodman-killed-himself-in-keystone-because-of-pot- edibles-family-says-6616258.

Roberts M, "Daniel Juarez's Stabbing Suicide Latest Death Linked to Marijuana Intoxication," *Westword*, May 19, 2015.

https://www.westword.com/news/daniel-juarezs-stabbing-suicide-latest-death-linked-to- marijuana-intoxication-6727165.

Russo M, Rifici C, Sessa E, D'Aleo G, Bramanti P, Calabrò RS. "Sativex-induced neurobehavioral effects: causal or concausal? A practical advice!" *DARU* 23, no. 1 (2015): 25. https://www.ncbi.nlm.nih.gov/pmc/articles/PMC4407789/pdf/40199_2015_Article_109.pdf.

Schauer GL, Peters EN. "Correlates and trends in youth co-use of marijuana and tobacco in the United States, 2005–2014." *Drug Alcohol Depend.* 185 (2018): 238-244. https://pubmed.ncbi.nlm.nih.gov/29471228/.

Sellers CM, Diaz-Valdes Iriarte A, Wyman Battalen A, O'Brien KHM. "Alcohol and marijuana use as daily predictors of suicide ideation and attempts among adolescents prior to psychiatric hospitalization." *Psychiatry Res.* 273 (2019): 672-677. https://www.sciencedirect.com/science/article/abs/pii/S0165178118323321?via%3Dihub.

Silins E, Horwood LJ, Patton GC, Fergusson DM, Olsson CA, Hutchinson DM, et al. "Young adult sequelae of adolescent cannabis use: an integrative analysis." *The Lancet Psychiatry* 1, no. 4 (2014): 286-93.

https://www.thelancet.com/journals/lanpsy/article/PIIS2215-0366(14)70307-4/fulltext.

Turner HA, Finkelhor D, Shattuck A, Hamby S. "Recent Victimization Exposure and Suicidal Ideation in Adolescents." *Arch Pediatr Adolesc Med*. 166, no. 12 (2012): 1149-54. https://jamanetwork.com/journals/ jamapediatrics/articlepdf/1384983/poa120051_1149_1154.pdf.

van Reekum R, Streiner DL, Conn DK. "Applying Bradford Hill's Criteria for Causation to Neuropsychiatry: Challenges and Opportunities." *J Neuropsychiatry Clin Neurosci*. 13, no. 3 (2001): 318-25. https://neuro. psychiatryonline.org/doi/pdf/10.1176/jnp.13.3.318.

Vijayakumar L, Phillips MR, Silverman MM, Gunnell D, Patel V, Chisholm D, Dua T, et al., "Suicide," in *Mental, Neurological, and Substance Use Disorders: Disease Control Priorities*, Third Edition (Volume 4). Washington (DC): The International Bank for Reconstruction and Development/The World Bank; Mar 14, 2016, chapter 9. https://www.ncbi.nlm.nih.gov/books/ NBK361942/?report=printable.

WHO, *Global Report on Trends in Prevalence of Tobacco Use, 2000-2025*, Third Edition, 2019. https://apps.who.int/iris/bitstream/ handle/10665/330221/9789240000032-eng.pdf.

Zammit S, Allebeck P, Andreasson S, Lundberg I, Lewis G. "Self-reported cannabis use as a risk factor for schizophrenia in Swedish conscripts of 1969: historical cohort study." *BMJ* 325, no. 7374 (2002): 1199.

https://www.ncbi.nlm.nih.gov/pmc/articles/PMC135490/pdf/1199.pdf.

GLOSSARY OF TERMS

AA – Alcoholics Anonymous

BP – bipolar

CBD – cannabidiol

CHS – cannabinoid hyperemesis syndrome

CIT – crisis intervention team

CIP – cannabis-induced psychosis

CUD – cannabis use disorder

DBT – dialectical behavior therapy

ED – emergency department

IOP – intensive outpatient program

NMS – neuroleptic malignant syndrome

PES – psychiatric emergency services

PHP – partial hospitalization program

POCCIP – parents of children with cannabis-induced psychosis

THC – delta-9-tetrahydrocannabinol

ACKNOWLEDGMENTS

MY GREATEST APPRECIATION goes to the 24 writers (one with two stories) who bravely shared their heartbreaking stories to make this book a reality. I honor you; I love you; and I thank you for working through your pain to try to save others. I know you shed many tears while writing your stories. We wrap our arms around you in understanding and comfort.

Our extreme gratitude goes to Dr. Christine Miller for writing and providing the two appendices in this book on the effects of THC on psychosis and suicidality. Dr. Miller has researched the causes of psychosis for 30 years in the academic setting, publishing 36 papers on neuroscience in peer-reviewed journals and books. Her specialty is molecular neuroscience (the study of molecular influences on brain function).

We're grateful to the hundreds more who have written to us to share how their children have been harmed by THC use. Thank you for speaking out! You can read their stories and submit yours at https://JohnnysAmbassadors.org/category/share-your-thc-story. We also recognize those who have lost their children due to the outcomes of THC use at https://JohnnysAmbassadors.org/memorial.

My gratitude goes to our volunteer editors, who helped our writers create and perfect their stories: Amy Wadsworth; Amy Turncliff; Angela

Williams Cherry; Ann S Eidson-Hunt; Carrie Chambers; Chris Norton; Cindy Perkins; Cindy Rosine Grogan; Daniel Pressello; Dominique McLerran; Elizabeth Henderson Stelling; Jan Typher; Jane Dvorak, APR, Fellow PRSA; Jen Douglas; Jennifer Lackey Newnam; Julie Potiker; June E Ramos; Kathleen Sheffield; Kathryn Hodge Matchett; Katie Klebaum; Kristi Lawrence; Kristie Andersen; Lara Anderson Miller; Laurie Gunderson; Linda Thrapp; Lisa Pea Bee; Lydia Gonzalez StJohn; Lynette Schick; Martha Han; Father Martin Nagy; Melanie Young; Nancy Hahn Henderson Stultz; Nancy Mueller; Pamela Less; Phaedra Brown; Shannon Lukei; Sheri E. Barnes; Sheri Wall; Sue Rhodehouse; Theresa Perkins Norton; Tracy Goodrich Truhan; and William Scott.

Thank you also to the thousands of Johnny's Ambassadors around the world who engage in our Facebook group, share our posts, and participate in our events. They share our mission to educate parents, teens, and communities about the dangers of today's potent THC products. Join our mailing list at https://JohnnysAmbassadors.org/blog. School leaders and community coalitions, please invite your teens to help us teach other teens at https://JohnnysAmbassadors.org/tagteam.

A huge thanks to our donors, whose financial support sustains our daily operations and projects. We literally wouldn't be able to do our important work without all of you.

Next, I thank God, who gave me this important mission to comfort me after the loss of Johnny. Every teen I talk to gives me joy and heals my soul. The Bible tells us to rejoice always, pray constantly, and give thanks in ALL circumstances. Jesus continues to lead me through this ordeal.

Our Christian faith teaches that once you ask Jesus into your heart, He never departs from you, and we are saved by grace through faith. Johnny had accepted Christ, so I know beyond a shadow of a doubt when he died, the Lord held him in His arms. Johnny is no longer tormented, and we will see him again when we leave this world to join Jesus in heaven. Even though our hearts are broken, God does give us something worth trusting in tough times: HIM.

Last, I thank YOU for reading this book. When you finish it, please help us sound the alarm about the dangers of youth THC misuse by sharing it with someone else. And then join us in our mission to educate parents, teens, and communities about the dangers of today's potent THC products (marijuana, dabs, vapes, and edibles) on adolescent brain development and their relationship with psychosis and suicide at https://community.JohnnysAmbassadors.org.

With gratitude and love,
Laura

ABOUT THE AUTHOR

THE TRUE STORIES IN THIS BOOK were written by 24 parents and compiled by Laura Stack. The stories are anonymous to protect the privacy of the children mentioned.

Laura Stack is Johnny Stack's mom and the founder and CEO of the nonprofit Johnny's Ambassadors Youth THC Prevention. In the business world, Laura was known by her professional moniker, The Productivity Pro®. For over 30 years, she has been a hall-of-fame professional speaker, corporate spokesperson for many major brands, and best-selling author of eight previous books on employee productivity.

On November 20, 2019, Laura suddenly acquired the undesired wisdom of knowing what it's like to lose one's child. Her 19-year-old son, Johnny, died by suicide after becoming psychotic from dabbing high-potency THC concentrates.

Laura's world took a 180. She filed for and received 501(c)(3) nonprofit status for Johnny's Ambassadors, Inc., with the mission to educate parents, teens, and communities about the dangers of today's potent THC products (marijuana, dabs, vapes, and edibles) on adolescent brain development and their relationship with psychosis and suicide.

Laura wrote the bestselling book about Johnny's life and death story, *The Dangerous Truth About Today's Marijuana: Johnny Stack's Life and*

Death Story. Described as a woman with unstoppable drive and unwavering purpose, Laura hopes to help other teens, parents, and all adults with teens in their lives by honestly and boldly sharing Johnny's story of his high-potency marijuana addiction, psychosis, and suicide.

The devastating loss of her child gives Laura a powerful voice and a platform for change. Laura sees it as her responsibility to share Johnny's warning to prevent other families from having to go through what she did and save other young lives from the harms of marijuana.

Laura now travels around the U.S. with her husband, speaking 200-plus times a year at school assemblies and prevention conferences. Her platform brings education about youth THC use, mental illness, and suicide. She presents in-person and virtual keynotes, breakout sessions, and training for parents, teens, schools, healthcare, antidrug coalitions, communities, and government agencies.

Laura is the recipient of the Drug-Free America Foundation's Moxie Award for protecting youth from substances, the Leadership in Advocacy Award from the National Speakers Association, and the American Association of Suicidology's Loss Survivor of the Year Award. Johnny's story has been told in *People* magazine, the *New York Times*, the *Wall Street Journal*, the *Epoch Times*, the *Ingraham Angle*, and on the *Untold Story with Martha MacCallum*, *PBS*, and *Dr. Phil*.

By sharing Johnny's own warning about marijuana, Laura is determined to start a movement to bring teen marijuana use, mental illness, and suicide into the spotlight and get them to #StopDabbing. There are now over 12,000 Johnny's Ambassadors sharing their stories and education to save others. Laura lives with her husband in south Denver, Colorado, and has two surviving adult children.

> *"Forge ahead despite your pain and give meaning to your loss."*
> —*Laura Stack*

CONNECT WITH LAURA STACK AND JOHNNY'S AMBASSADORS

- Phone: (303) 471-7401
- Email: Laura@JohnnysAmbassadors.org
- Website: https://JohnnysAmbassadors.org
- Get help for a child using THC: https://JohnnysAmbassadors. org/parents
- Speaking inquiries (virtual and in person): https:// JohnnysAmbassadors.org/speaking
- X: https://twitter.com/JohnnyKStack
- Public Facebook prevention group: https://www.facebook.com/ groups/JohnnysAmbassadors
- Private Facebook group for Parents of Children with Cannabis-Induced Psychosis (POCCIP): https://www.facebook.com/ groups/POCCIP
- Facebook group for THC child loss (by invitation only): https:// www.facebook.com/groups/thcdeath
- LinkedIn: https://www.linkedin.com/in/laurastack
- YouTube: https://www.youtube.com/JohnnysAmbassadors

Made in United States
North Haven, CT
14 May 2024

52494187R00143